TouchPoints
of Hope

GOD'S ANSWERS FOR

YOUR DAILY NEEDS

Tyndale House Publishers, Inc.
Wheaton, Illinois

Visit Tyndale's exciting Web site at www.tyndale.com

TouchPoints of Hope

General Editors: Ronald A. Beers and V. Gilbert Beers

Managing editor: Sanford D. Hull

Contributing writers: V. Gilbert Beers, Ronald A. Beers, Brian R. Coffey, Jonathan D. Gray, Shawn A. Harrison, Sanford D. Hull, Rhonda K. O'Brien, Douglas J. Rumford.

Designed by Beth Sparkman

Edited by Linda K. Taylor

ISBN 0-8423-4229-X

Printed in the United States of America

09   08   07   06   05   04   03
8   7   6   5   4   3   2   1

PREFACE

Psalm 119:111, 162 *Your decrees are my treasure; they are truly my heart's delight. . . . I rejoice in your word like one who finds a great treasure.*

Psalm 119: 91, 160 *Your laws remain true today, for everything serves your plans. . . . All your words are true; all your just laws will stand forever.*

Psalm 119:105 *Your word is a lamp for my feet and a light for my path.*

What a treasure we have in God's Word! In its pages you can find words of hope for any situation, any concern, and any trial. Sometimes, however, it's difficult to find the verse you need when you need it. That's why we've written this book—to touch your heart with hope from God's Word, to help you find the verses you need when you need them.

In this book you will find more than one hundred "touchpoints," topics for daily living. Each topic is listed alphabetically, with several questions, Scripture passages, and comments addressing each topic. In the index at the back, you will find a complete listing of all the topics for quick reference. You can read through this book page by page or use it as a reference guide for topics of particular interest to you.

Although we could not cover all topics, questions, and Scriptures related to the subject of this book, our prayer is that you will continue to search God's Word deliberately and diligently. May you find God's answers, for he longs to be your daily guide. Enjoy your treasure hunt!

—THE EDITORS

2 Timothy 3:16-17 *All Scripture is inspired by God and is useful to teach us what is true and to make us realize what is wrong in our lives. It straightens us out and teaches us to do what is right. It is God's way of preparing us in every way, fully equipped for every good thing God wants us to do.*

Abandonment

Will God abandon me during my difficult times?

Psalm 9:10 _Those who know your name trust in you, for you, O Lord, have never abandoned anyone who searches for you._

Psalm 27:10 _Even if my father and mother abandon me, the Lord will hold me close._

John 14:16 _And I will ask the Father, and he will give you another Counselor, who will never leave you._

2 Corinthians 4:9 _We are hunted down, but God never abandons us. We get knocked down, but we get up again and keep going._

A seeking God and a seeking person are always sure to find each other. God will never abandon a seeking person. When you face difficult times, you can trust that God has not abandoned you. You may feel alone, but God is there.

1

Other people have abandoned me—why not God?

Genesis 37:28 *When the traders came by, his brothers pulled Joseph out of the pit and sold him for twenty pieces of silver.*

Genesis 39:3 *The Lord was with Joseph, giving him success in everything he did.*
You may feel like everyone is against you; you may carry the hurt that others have inflicted on you. But God is always for you because he loves you with a deep and lasting love. He will always be with you.

Does my suffering mean that God has abandoned me?

1 Peter 5:10 *After you have suffered a little while, he will restore, support, and strengthen you, and he will place you on a firm foundation.*
You may feel alone in your suffering, but God has compassion on you and promises that an eternal reward is waiting for you.

PROMISE FROM GOD: Hebrews 13:5 *I will never fail you. I will never forsake you.*

Absence

Why do I sometimes feel that God is absent?

Psalm 10:1 *O Lord, why do you stand so far away? Why do you hide when I need you the most?*

The greater our troubles, the farther away God sometimes seems to be. In your darkest hour, you may feel that God is hiding. Then you must have faith in his promises to always be with you.

Psalm 13:1-2 *O Lord, how long will you forget me? Forever? How long will you look the other way? How long must I struggle with anguish in my soul, with sorrow in my heart every day? How long will my enemies have the upper hand?*
Even faithful and godly King David, writer of this psalm, sometimes felt that God was absent. Do not assume that you are spiritually deficient because you feel as if God is far away. Don't trust your feelings; trust God's promises.

Is God absent in my times of intense pain and loneliness?

Psalm 139:7, 9-10 *I can never escape from your spirit! I can never get away from your presence! . . . If I ride the wings of the morning, if I dwell by the farthest oceans, even there your hand will guide me and your strength will support me.*

Psalm 23:4 *Even when I walk through the dark valley of death, I will not be afraid, for you are close beside me.*
God never promised a life free from sorrow, but he does promise to be with us even in our darkest moments. He does not promise to take us around the dark valley, but he does promise to walk with

3

us through it. This truth does not make these moments easy, but it enables us to move through them without fear. When you walk through the valley of suffering, sorrow, or loneliness, remember that God is close beside you.

PROMISE FROM GOD: Matthew 28:20 *Be sure of this: I am with you always, even to the end of the age.*

Abuse

How do I heal the wounds of abuse?

Ephesians 4:31 *Get rid of all bitterness, rage, anger, harsh words, and slander, as well as all types of malicious behavior.*
Recognize that resentment, bitterness, and desire for revenge will only poison your own soul. Your hurt is real, but you must leave it with God. He will bring justice in his way in his time.

Colossians 3:13 *Remember, the Lord forgave you, so you must forgive others.*
This is difficult, but important. If you refuse to forgive, you will only be hurting yourself. Remember that you did not deserve forgiveness, but Jesus forgave you by grace; likewise, an abuser does not deserve your forgiveness, but you can choose to forgive anyway. When you forgive, you are *not* saying the hurt isn't real, or that the

event didn't matter, or that you will put yourself in a position where you might be harmed again. Leave your hurt with God, and allow him to comfort you and heal you.

Philippians 4:8 *Fix your thoughts on what is true and honorable and right. Think about things that are pure and lovely and admirable. Think about things that are excellent and worthy of praise.* As you fill your mind with thoughts about God, there is less room, and less time, to dwell on the past. Focus on the future and on all God's promises to you.

Will God forgive a person who is guilty of abuse?

Acts 2:21 *And anyone who calls on the name of the Lord will be saved.*

2 Chronicles 33:6, 13 *Manasseh even sacrificed his own sons in the fire in the valley of the son of Hinnom. . . . When he prayed, the Lord listened to him and was moved by his request for help.*
Manasseh was the most wicked king in Judah's history, abusive to the point of burning his own sons on an altar. Later in life, however, he sought God's forgiveness and God did forgive him, transforming him into a man who did great things for his nation. No sinner is too wicked for God to love; no sin is too vile for God to forgive.

5

PROMISE FROM GOD: Psalm 34:18 *The Lord is close to the brokenhearted; he rescues those who are crushed in spirit.*

Acceptance

I feel so unworthy—does God really accept me?

Romans 5:8 *But God showed his great love for us by sending Christ to die for us while we were still sinners.*

1 Timothy 1:15 *This is a true saying, and everyone should believe it: Christ Jesus came into the world to save sinners—and I was the worst of them all.*

God loves you—period. You are worth so much to God that he sent Jesus to earth for you.

Do I have to earn God's acceptance?

Romans 3:27 *Can we boast, then, that we have done anything to be accepted by God? No, because our acquittal is not based on our good deeds. It is based on our faith.*

No one can *earn* God's acceptance. Nothing we do could ever compensate for our sin. The only way to be accepted by God is to believe that his Son, Jesus, died for your sins so that you could be free to enjoy eternal life with him. When you accept his forgiveness and let him be Lord of your life, he completely accepts you into his presence. It's that simple.

What should I do when other people don't accept me?

Psalm 27:10 *Even if my mother and my father abandon me, the Lord will hold me close.*
Remember that God's love endures even when people are fickle or cruel.

Galatians 2:20 *The Son of God . . . loved me and gave himself for me.*
Your value is not determined by the opinions of others. You are a unique creation of God and you are redeemed through the death of God's Son. This divine assessment of your great worth is always true, regardless of how people treat you.

How can I accept all of life's circumstances that come my way?

Job 2:10 *But Job replied, ". . . Should we accept only good things from the hand of God and never anything bad?"*

Luke 1:38 *Mary responded, "I am the Lord's servant, and I am willing to accept whatever he wants. May everything you have said come true."*

Hebrews 10:34 *You suffered along with those who were thrown into jail. When all you owned was taken from you, you accepted it with joy. You knew*

you had better things waiting for you in eternity.
Accepting your circumstances doesn't mean you
have to like them. By keeping an eternal perspective, however, you can learn from and grow
through the difficult times. When you accept
what comes from God's hand, you can trust that
he has something to teach you through whatever
comes your way. Remember that difficult circumstances will not follow you to heaven—one day,
you will be in a place where there will be no
more tears or sorrow. One day, God will make
all things right.

PROMISE FROM GOD: Galatians
4 : 3 1 *So, dear brothers and sisters, we are not
children of the slave woman, obligated to the law.
We are children of the free woman, acceptable to God
because of our faith.*

Accusations

Where do accusations come from?

Zechariah 3:1 *Then the angel showed me Jeshua
the high priest standing before the angel of the Lord.
Satan was there at the angel's right hand, accusing
Jeshua of many things.*

Job 2:1 *One day the angels came again to present
themselves before the Lord, and Satan the Accuser*

8

came with them.

Revelation 12:9-10 *This great dragon—the ancient serpent called the Devil, or Satan, the one deceiving the whole world—was thrown down to the earth with all his angels. Then I heard a loud voice shouting across the heavens, "It has happened at last . . . the Accuser has been thrown down to earth— the one who accused our brothers and sisters before our God day and night."*

Satan is the ultimate false accuser. He will try to accuse you of many things; he will try to make you doubt your faith, your salvation, or your acceptance by God. That's when you must turn back to God's promises and focus on his truth.

John 8:9 *When the accusers heard this, they slipped away one by one, beginning with the oldest, until only Jesus was left in the middle of the crowd with the woman.*

Sometimes accusation can come from your conscience. You would do well to listen and then seek God. He may be trying to point out sin in your life so that you can repent, be free, and enjoy closer fellowship with him.

Deuteronomy 19:16 *If a malicious witness comes forward and accuses someone of a crime . . .*

Ezra 4:6 *Years later when Xerxes began his reign, the enemies of Judah wrote him a letter of accusation against the people of Judah and Jerusalem.*

9

Sometimes accusation comes from those who dislike us. Sometimes believers are victims of false accusations. In those times, we must entrust ourselves to God and his truth.

How should I respond to accusations against me?

Psalm 35:20-24 *They don't talk of peace; they plot against innocent people who are minding their own business. They shout that they have seen me doing wrong. "Aha," they say. "Aha! With our own eyes we saw him do it!" O Lord, you know all about this. . . . Rise to my defense! Take up my case, my God and my Lord. Declare me "not guilty," O Lord my God, for you give justice.*
Realize that God has full knowledge of the accusation and the truth, and that he has the authority and ability to handle the situation. If you are innocent, leave justice with God.

Nehemiah 6:8-9 *My reply was, "You know you are lying. There is no truth in any part of your story." They were just trying to intimidate us, imagining that they could break our resolve and stop the work. So I prayed for strength to continue the work.*
Don't become so focused on the accusation that you forget about God. Take the matter to him and get strength from him.

Genesis 3:11-13 *"Who told you that you were naked?" the Lord God asked. "Have you eaten the fruit I commanded you not to eat?" "Yes," Adam admitted, "but it was the woman you gave me who brought me the fruit, and I ate it." Then the Lord God asked the woman, "How could you do such a thing?" "The serpent tricked me," she replied. "That's why I ate it."*

Hosea 4:4 *Don't point your finger at someone else and try to pass the blame! Look, you priests, my complaint is with you!*
It is so easy to blame others. There are times when we should accept the blame that is rightfully ours. If an accusation against you is true, you need to deal with it appropriately, making restitution or offering repentance.

Luke 12:11-12 *And when you are brought to trial in the synagogues and before rulers and authorities, don't worry about what to say in your defense, for the Holy Spirit will teach you what needs to be said even as you are standing there.*

Be sensitive to the Holy Spirit's guidance in responding to accusations. He may give you help you never thought possible.

1 Peter 3:14 *But even if you suffer for doing what is right, God will reward you for it. So don't be afraid and don't worry.*
Although false accusations sometimes lead to unjust earthly punishments, the ultimate Judge,

holding both punishments and rewards, is God. As the just Judge, God will always bring justice. Sometimes his justice is swift. Sometimes it is deferred beyond this earth.

1 Peter 2:12, 15 *Be careful how you live among your unbelieving neighbors. Even if they accuse you of doing wrong, they will see your honorable behavior, and they will believe and give honor to God when he comes to judge the world. . . . It is God's will that your good lives should silence those who make foolish accusations against you.* Continue to live an honorable life before your accusers. Christlikeness is magnetic. You may attract the accuser to the Savior.

PROMISE FROM GOD: Romans 8:33-34 *Who dares accuse us whom God has chosen for his own? Will God? No! He is the one who has given us right standing with himself. Who then will condemn us? Will Christ Jesus? No, for he is the one who died for us and was raised to life for us and is sitting at the place of highest honor next to God, pleading for us.*

Addiction

Can addiction include more than substance abuse?

2 Peter 2:19 *[These false teachers] promise free-*

dom, but they themselves are slaves to sin and corruption. For you are a slave to whatever controls you. The key to addiction is control. Whenever we have a master, we are slaves. Addiction is relinquishing ourselves to the control of something or someone else.

Luke 1:37 *For nothing is impossible with God.* In order to overcome your addiction, you must believe it is possible. You will have this confidence when you recognize the greatness of God's power at work in you and for you.

Ecclesiastes 4:9-10, 12 *Two people can accomplish more than twice as much as one; they get a better return on their labor. If one person falls, the other can reach out and help. But people who are alone when they fall are in real trouble. . . . A person standing alone can be attacked and defeated, but two can stand back-to-back and conquer. Three are even better, for a triple-braided cord is not easily broken.* It is almost impossible to overcome addiction by yourself. You need the consistent support of other people who love you, tell you the truth, and hold you accountable. Participating in some sort of addiction recovery support group is important, perhaps even essential, in order to overcome an addiction.

PROMISE FROM GOD: John 8:36 *So if the Son sets you free, you will indeed be free.*

Adversity

Is God listening when I cry out because of my afflictions or troubles? Does he really hear and does he care?

Jonah 2:2 *I cried out to the Lord in my great trouble, and he answered me. I called to you from the world of the dead, and Lord, you heard me!*
God's hot line is always open. There is never a busy signal, for he is never too busy with anything—even managing the world—to listen to your every need. God has both a listening ear and a caring heart.

It's hard for me to believe that God actually sends adversity into my life. Don't troubles just happen?

Deuteronomy 28:20 *The Lord himself will send against you curses, confusion, and disillusionment . . . for doing evil and forsaking me.*

Jeremiah 21:14 *"I myself will punish you for your sinfulness," says the Lord.*

Hosea 4:9 *So now I will punish both priests and people for all their wicked deeds.*
Troubles do often "just happen" because we live in a sinful world, and God usually allows the cycle of sin to play itself out (for now). But just as a loving parent brings adversity into the life

of a child through discipline, God may also bring adversity into our lives to correct us when we do wrong. This is for our benefit, not harm. God may also bring difficulties into our lives to strengthen us and prepare us for life ahead. When you face adversity, stay close to God. Ask him to show you if the adversity is a form of discipline, or if it is simply part of living in a sinful world.

Does God enjoy punishing me or sending troubles to me?

Lamentations 3:33 *He does not enjoy hurting people or causing them sorrow.*

Romans 5:8 *But God showed his great love for us by sending Christ to die for us while we were still sinners.*

God's love for us is pure and intense; he does not want to see us suffer! But our suffering would be worse if he did not sometimes correct us. Remember that in your suffering, God suffers with you—wanting you to turn back to him, to trust him, to learn from him.

Will being faithful to God spare me from adversity?

1 Peter 2:21 *This suffering is all part of what God has called you to. Christ, who suffered for you, is your example.*

Satan is our enemy, and he will try to stop us from following God. There are also people

who are opposed to what is good and right.
Adversity may be a sign that you are being faithful to God.

Is there any way I can avoid trouble and adversity?

James 1:2-3 *Whenever trouble comes your way, let it be an opportunity for joy. For when your faith is tested, your endurance has a chance to grow.*

2 Corinthians 4:8 *We are pressed on every side by troubles, but we are not crushed and broken.* Avoiding adversity may not be best for you. Though adversity may bruise you, it also can build you up and strengthen your faith.

Proverbs 16:17 *The path of the upright leads away from evil; whoever follows that path is safe.*

Colossians 3:5 *So put to death the sinful, earthly things lurking within you. Have nothing to do with sexual sin, impurity, lust, and shameful desires. Don't be greedy for the good things of this life, for that is idolatry.*

Proverbs 14:16 *The wise are cautious and avoid danger; fools plunge ahead with great confidence.* The consequences of sin often bring unneeded adversity into our lives. By obeying God's Word, we can avoid many kinds of self-inflicted adversity.

Are there other benefits to adversity?

1 Peter 4:1, 13 *If you are willing to suffer*

for Christ, you have decided to stop sinning. . . .
These trials will make you partners with Christ in
his suffering.
Adversity helps us understand Christ better
because he suffered for us. This deepens our
relationship with him.

PROMISES FROM GOD: Psalm
46:1 *God is our refuge and strength, always ready*
to help in times of trouble.

Isaiah 43:2-3 *When you go through deep waters*
and great trouble, I will be with you. . . . For I am the
Lord, your God.

Psalm 9:12 *He does not ignore those who cry*
to him for help.

Aging/Old Age

What are some of the benefits of old age?
Proverbs 20:29 *The glory of the young is their*
strength; the gray hair of experience is the splendor
of the old.
A benefit of old age is the wisdom that can come
from a lifetime of experience.

Psalm 71:18 *Now that I am old and gray, do not*
abandon me, O God. Let me proclaim your power to
this new generation, your mighty miracles to all who
come after me.

17

Old age affords the opportunity to pass on to the next generation the lessons of a lifetime of experiencing God's faithfulness and growing spiritually.

I'm getting up in years. Can God still use me?

Genesis 12:4 *So Abram departed as the Lord had instructed him, and Lot went with him. Abram was seventy-five years old when he left Haran.*

Deuteronomy 32:7 *Remember the days of long ago; think about the generations past. Ask your father and he will inform you. Inquire of your elders, and they will tell you.*

Older people have seen God's hand in their lives over many years. What a privilege you have to share this perspective with those who are younger, strengthening their faith with evidence of God's faithfulness.

Titus 2:2-5 *Teach the older men to exercise self-control, to be worthy of respect, and to live wisely. They must have strong faith and be filled with love and patience. Similarly, teach the older women to live in a way that is appropriate for someone serving the Lord. They must not go around speaking evil of others and must not be heavy drinkers. Instead, they should teach others what is good. These older women must train the younger women to love their husbands and their children, to live wisely and be pure, to take care of their homes, to do good, and to be submissive to their husbands. Then they will not bring shame on the word of God.*

Older people are uniquely equipped to be teachers of God's ways of living. With age comes great responsibility to be a good example and a good teacher to those coming behind you.

What are some responsibilities of younger people toward older people?

Leviticus 19:32 *Show your fear of God by standing up in the presence of elderly people and showing respect for the aged. I am the Lord.*

Younger people are to respect older people.

Exodus 20:12 *Honor your father and mother. Then you will live a long, full life in the land the Lord your God will give you.*

Younger people are to honor their parents.

1 Peter 5:5 *You younger men, accept the authority of the elders. And all of you, serve each other in humility, for "God sets himself against the proud, but he shows favor to the humble."*

Younger people are to accept the authority of older people and serve them humbly.

PROMISE FROM GOD: Isaiah 46:4 *I will be your God throughout your lifetime—until your hair is white with age. I made you, and I will care for you. I will carry you along and save you.*

Apathy

What can I do when I am feeling apathetic?

Psalm 119:83 *I am shriveled like a wineskin in smoke, exhausted with waiting. But I cling to your principles and obey them.*

Obey God's commands even when you don't feel like it—in fact, even when you don't feel like doing anything. Such obedience keeps you close to God and prevents apathy from wreaking havoc in your life. When you obey, the feeling of apathy will pass.

Acts 16:25 *Around midnight, Paul and Silas were praying and singing hymns to God, and the other prisoners were listening.*

Instead of letting adversity create apathy, worship God through prayer and song, and stay connected with Christian friends. You may not feel like doing this, but choose to do it anyway and your efforts will bear fruit. Prayer and praise to God help cure apathy.

Proverbs 20:13 *If you love sleep, you will end in poverty. Keep your eyes open, and there will be plenty to eat!*

Understanding the negative consequences of apathy can motivate you to action.

Proverbs 19:3 *People ruin their lives by their own foolishness and then are angry at the Lord.*

Taking responsibility for your own actions and attitudes—not seeing yourself as a victim of someone or something—can be a crucial step to overcoming apathy.

PROMISE FROM GOD: 2 Timothy 1 : 7 *God has not given us a spirit of fear and timidity, but of power, love, and self-discipline.*

Assurance

Where can I find assurance amid the uncertainties of life?

Psalm 118:8-9 *It is better to trust the Lord than to put confidence in people. It is better to trust the Lord than to put confidence in princes.*

Psalm 40:4 *Oh, the joys of those who trust the Lord, who have no confidence in the proud, or in those who worship idols.*

1 Peter 1:21 *Through Christ you have come to trust in God. And because God raised Christ from the dead and gave him great glory, your faith and hope can be placed confidently in God.*
Though it is good and necessary to trust others, God is the only one in whom we can completely trust without fear of disappointment. You can have complete assurance that what he says is true and what he does is reliable. People, who are not

perfect, will sometimes fail you; God, who is perfect, will never fail you. The world is filled with uncertainty, but you can trust in God's sure promises.

Hebrews 10:22 *Let us go right into the presence of God, with true hearts fully trusting him. For our evil consciences have been sprinkled with Christ's blood to make us clean, and our bodies have been washed with pure water.*
You can approach God knowing that he gladly welcomes you and will never reject you. God will never say, "Sorry, I don't have time for you," or "Sorry, don't bother me." He always listens, always hears, always loves, is always there.

How can I increase my confidence in God's assurance?

Psalm 108:1 *My heart is confident in you, O God; no wonder I can sing your praises! Wake up, my soul!*
Praise will increase your assurance. As you focus on the Lord instead of your problems or fears, your confidence in him will increase.

Psalm 40:1, 5 *I waited patiently for the Lord to help me, and he turned to me and heard my cry. . . . O Lord my God, you have done many miracles for us. Your plans for us are too numerous to list.*
As you depend on God in your everyday life, God develops a track record that makes you more confident as you face today's challenges.

What God has done assures you of what he will continue to do.

How can I be sure of God's love for me?

Lamentations 3:22-23 *The unfailing love of the Lord never ends! By his mercies we have been kept from complete destruction. Great is his faithfulness; his mercies begin afresh each day.*

Romans 5:8 *But God showed his great love for us by sending Christ to die for us while we were still sinners.*

Romans 8:35, 38-39 *Can anything ever separate us from Christ's love? Does it mean he no longer loves us if we have trouble or calamity, or are persecuted, or are hungry or cold or in danger or threatened with death? . . . And I am convinced that nothing can ever separate us from his love. Death can't, and life can't. The angels can't, and the demons can't. Our fears for today, our worries about tomorrow, and even the powers of hell can't keep God's love away. Whether we are high above the sky or in the deepest ocean, nothing in all creation will ever be able to separate us from the love of God that is revealed in Christ Jesus our Lord.*

You can have full assurance in God's love because God *is* love. His love is woven into his character. Love is not merely something God does; love is who he is. Nothing can ever separate you from God's love.

How can I be sure of God's promises for me?

Psalm 146:6 *He is the one who made heaven and earth, the sea, and everything in them. He is the one who keeps every promise forever.*

Hebrews 6:18 *God has given us both his promise and his oath. These two things are unchangeable because it is impossible for God to lie. Therefore, we who have fled to him for refuge can take new courage, for we can hold on to his promise with confidence.* You can have assurance in God's promises because God is truth. He cannot and does not lie.

Psalm 105:42 *For he remembered his sacred promise to Abraham his servant.*

Romans 4:20-21 *Abraham never wavered in believing God's promise. In fact, his faith grew stronger, and in this he brought glory to God. He was absolutely convinced that God was able to do anything he promised.*

2 Chronicles 6:4 *Blessed be the Lord, the God of Israel, who has kept the promise he made to my father, David.*

2 Corinthians 1:20 *For all of God's promises have been fulfilled in him. That is why we say "Amen" when we give glory to God through Christ.* Fulfilled prophecies and historical examples are evidence of God's ability to keep his promises. If we trust people because we have seen their

track record over a few years, certainly we can trust God because he has a spotless track record from the beginning of time. Because he has always kept his promises, you can trust that he will continue to keep his promises.

What are some ways to be certain I know Jesus as my Savior and Lord?

Romans 10:9 *For if you confess with your mouth that Jesus is Lord and believe in your heart that God raised him from the dead, you will be saved.*

Acts 2:21 *And anyone who calls on the name of the Lord will be saved.*

Hebrews 3:14 *For if we are faithful to the end, trusting God just as firmly as when we first believed, we will share in all that belongs to Christ.*
If you believe that Jesus saves you from sin, you confess your sins to him, and you acknowledge that he is Lord of all, then you are saved. Jesus is your Savior and Lord. How do you know? Because God promised, and God always keeps his promises. Although your relationship with Jesus as Savior and Lord of your life begins at a moment in time, you should continue an active, daily trust in Jesus Christ throughout your life.

1 John 3:24 *Those who obey God's command-ments live in fellowship with him, and he with them. And we know he lives in us because the Holy Spirit lives in us.*

1 J o h n 4 : 1 3 *And God has given us his Spirit as proof that we live in him and he in us.*
God gave you his Holy Spirit to give you assurance of your relationship with him.

1 J o h n 5 : 1 8 *We know that those who have become part of God's family do not make a practice of sinning, for God's Son holds them securely, and the evil one cannot get his hands on them.*
When Jesus becomes your Savior and Lord, you begin a lifestyle of obedience. When Jesus saves you, he changes all of you, not just your testimony. Is your life different than it was before you were saved? If so, you can see that God has been at work in you.

1 J o h n 3 : 1 4 , 1 7 *If we love our Christian brothers and sisters, it proves that we have passed from death to eternal life. But a person who has no love is still dead. . . . But if anyone has enough money to live well and sees a brother or sister in need and refuses to help—how can God's love be in that person?*
Love for others is evidence of your relationship with Jesus as your Savior and Lord. As a tree produces fruit, so your life produces good things—not the least of which is love. When people see the fruit of love, they recognize that the Holy Spirit controls your character.

PROMISE FROM GOD: J e r e m i a h
1 7 : 7 - 8 *Blessed are those who trust in the Lord*

and have made the Lord their hope and confidence. They are like trees planted along a riverbank, with roots that reach deep into the water. Such trees are not bothered by the heat or worried by long months of drought. Their leaves stay green, and they go right on producing delicious fruit.

Betrayal

What should I do when I feel betrayed?

Matthew 26:45 *Look, the time has come. I, the Son of Man, am betrayed into the hands of sinners.*
It is important to recognize that betrayal is an inevitable part of the human experience. Even Jesus was betrayed. This doesn't make being betrayed easy, but it helps you realize that it doesn't mean there is something wrong with you.

Hebrews 4:15 *This High Priest of ours understands our weaknesses.*
There is comfort in the fact that Jesus was betrayed. He knows firsthand your pain. He who has the power to help you has experienced your hurt himself.

Genesis 33:4, 9-10 *Then Esau ran to meet him and embraced him affectionately and kissed him. Both of them were in tears. . . . "Brother, I have plenty," Esau answered. "Keep what you have."*

"No, please accept them," Jacob said, *"for what a relief it is to see your friendly smile. It is like seeing the smile of God!"*

You are called to forgive, even when someone betrays you. Forgiveness is the only escape from the downward spiral of retaliation and revenge.

Jeremiah 12:6 *Even your own brothers, members of your own family, have turned on you. They have plotted, raising a cry against you. Do not trust them, no matter how pleasantly they speak.*

When you realize that you cannot trust a particular person, acting wisely includes taking steps to keep from getting hurt again. You can avoid revenge and grant forgiveness while still exercising prudent self-protection.

Genesis 50:19-21 *But Joseph told them, "Don't be afraid of me. Am I God, to judge and punish you? As far as I am concerned, God turned into good what you meant for evil. He brought me to the high position I have today so I could save the lives of many people. No, don't be afraid. Indeed, I myself will take care of you and your families." And he spoke very kindly to them, reassuring them.*

Recognize God's hand in your life. Even when someone sins against you, such as betraying you, God can pick up the pieces and make something good from them.

Psalm 118:8 *It is better to trust the Lord than to put confidence in people.*

People may trample on your trust, but the Lord will never betray you.

PROMISE FROM GOD: Isaiah 54:10 *"For the mountains may depart and the hills disappear, but even then I will remain loyal to you. My covenant of blessing will never be broken," says the Lord, who has mercy on you.*

$\mathcal{B}\,i\,t\,t\,e\,r\,n\,e\,s\,s$

What are some of the causes of bitter feelings?

Genesis 27:41 *Esau hated Jacob because he had stolen his blessing.*

Esther 5:9 *What a happy man Haman was as he left the banquet! But when he saw Mordecai sitting at the gate, not standing up or trembling nervously before him, he was furious.*
Bitterness comes when we resent the blessings others have that we do not have.

Hebrews 12:15 *Watch out that no bitter root of unbelief rises up among you, for whenever it springs up, many are corrupted by its poison.*
Bitterness comes by forgetting God's grace. Bitterness is like a poison that affects not only us, but everyone around us.

29

Ecclesiastes 2:17 *So now I hate life because everything done here under the sun is so irrational. Everything is meaningless, like chasing the wind.*

Proverbs 19:3 *People ruin their lives by their own foolishness and then are angry at the Lord.* Practicing sin cultivates the fruits of sin—emptiness, bitterness, foolishness, and a sense of meaningless activity.

What is the result of unresolved bitterness?

Job 5:2 *Surely resentment destroys the fool, and jealousy kills the simple.*

Proverbs 27:3 *A stone is heavy and sand is weighty, but the resentment caused by a fool is heavier than both.*
Unresolved bitterness leads to hatred, anger, jealousy, and revenge. It can keep us from fellowship with God and others and blocks us from noticing God's blessings.

How do I deal with bitterness toward others?

Mark 11:25 *But when you are praying, first forgive anyone you are holding a grudge against, so that your Father in heaven will forgive your sins, too.*
Forgiveness lifts burdens, cancels debts, and frees you from chains of bitterness.

How can I help a bitter person?

2 Corinthians 2:7 *Now it is time to forgive*

*him and comfort him. Otherwise he may become so
discouraged that he won't be able to recover.*
There are times when simple forgiveness can
relieve a lifetime of bitterness. Recovery from
acute bitterness may be as complex as the reasons
for the bitterness, but it may also be as simple as
three spoken words: "I forgive you."

PROMISE FROM GOD: Titus 1:15
Everything is pure to those whose hearts are pure.

Blessings

How can I get God's blessings?
Ephesians 1:3 *How we praise God, the Father
of our Lord Jesus Christ, who has blessed us with
every spiritual blessing in the heavenly realms
because we belong to Christ.*
God's blessings are gifts of his grace. You should
never try to earn what can only be given. You
already have God's blessings because you are his
child.

Psalm 128:1 *How happy are those who fear the
Lord—all who follow his ways!*

Jeremiah 17:7 *Blessed are those who trust in
the Lord and have made the Lord their hope and
confidence.*

The more you trust and obey God, the more you will experience the blessings he gives.

How many blessings does God send my way?

Psalm 139:17-18 *How precious are your thoughts about me, O God! They are innumerable! I can't even count them.*

God's blessings are too many to count or even mention. His blessings come to you every day, in every conceivable form.

Numbers 6:24-26 *May the Lord bless you and protect you. May the Lord smile on you and be gracious to you. May the Lord show you his favor and give you his peace.*

Success and prosperity are not the most common blessings from God. Rather peace, comfort, joy, fellowship with God, hope, and eternal life with him are the best blessings of all—and they have been promised to you.

If God promises to bless his people, why is life sometimes so hard?

Acts 5:41 *The apostles left the high council rejoicing that God had counted them worthy to suffer dishonor for the name of Jesus.*

James 1:12 *God blesses the people who patiently endure testing.*

Sometimes the greatest blessings come out of

suffering or persecution because these trials deepen your relationship with the Lord, which is the greatest blessing of all.

Why is it important for me to thank God for my blessings?

Psalm 92:1-2 *It is good to give thanks to the Lord, . . . to proclaim your unfailing love in the morning, your faithfulness in the evening.*
God has given you far more than you will ever realize—all of it undeserved, all of it given freely because of his love for you. Thank him for this before you become ungrateful and lose out on all he has yet to offer. If a blessing is worth receiving, it is worth your thanksgiving.

What responsibilities come with God's blessings?

Deuteronomy 16:17 *All must give as they are able, according to the blessings given to them by the Lord your God.*

Matthew 10:8 *Give as freely as you have received!*
As God blesses you, you are to bless others. Receiving and giving go hand in hand.

How can I be a blessing to others?

Galatians 5:22-23 *When the Holy Spirit controls our lives, he will produce this kind of fruit in us: love, joy, peace, patience, kindness, goodness,*

faithfulness, gentleness, and self-control.
As you share the fruit of the Holy Spirit with
others, you will be both blessed and a blessing.

Romans 1:11-12 *For I long to visit you so I can
share a spiritual blessing with you that will help you
grow strong in the Lord. I'm eager to encourage you
in your faith, but I also want to be encouraged by
yours. In this way, each of us will be a blessing to
the other.*

2 Corinthians 2:14 *But thanks be to God,
who made us his captives and leads us along in
Christ's triumphal procession. Now wherever we go
he uses us to tell others about the Lord and to spread
the Good News like a sweet perfume.*
As you share the blessings God has poured on
you, you bless others as well. Encouraging others
with God's Good News is one of the most rewarding of his blessings.

PROMISE FROM GOD Psalm 84:11
*No good thing will the Lord withhold from those who
do what is right.*

Brokenhearted

(*see also* ENCOURAGEMENT or GRIEF or
SORROW)

**How does God respond to the
brokenhearted?**

Psalm 34:18 *The Lord is close to the broken-hearted; he rescues those who are crushed in spirit.*

Lamentations 3:32 *Though he brings grief, he also shows compassion according to the greatness of his unfailing love.*

Psalm 10:17 *Lord, you know the hopes of the helpless. Surely you will listen to their cries and comfort them.*

Isaiah 51:12 *I, even I, am the one who comforts you. So why are you afraid of mere humans, who wither like the grass and disappear?*

Psalm 147:3 *He heals the brokenhearted, binding up their wounds.*

Matthew 5:4 *God blesses those who mourn, for they will be comforted.*

The Lord comforts the brokenhearted by his presence, his compassion, his listening, his love, his healing, his encouragement, and his blessing. What more do any of us need?

What should I do when I am brokenhearted?

Psalm 130:1 *From the depths of despair, O Lord, I call for your help.*

Call to the Lord for his help. Be honest with your feelings. He who made you can heal your broken heart.

Psalm 119:28, 50, 52, 92 *I weep with grief;*
encourage me by your word. . . . Your promise revives
me; it comforts me in all my troubles. . . . I meditate
on your age-old laws; O Lord, they comfort me. . . .
If your law hadn't sustained me with joy, I would
have died in my misery.

Psalm 19:8 *The commandments of the Lord are*
right, bringing joy to the heart. The commands of the
Lord are clear, giving insight to life.
Look to the Word of God for help. Meditate on
God's character, promises, and commitment to
you. He who created the universe by his word
can re-create a new spirit within you.

Ecclesiastes 3:4 *A time to cry and a time*
to laugh. A time to grieve and a time to dance.

2 Corinthians 2:4 *How painful it was to write*
that letter! Heartbroken, I cried over it. I didn't want
to hurt you, but I wanted you to know how very much
I love you.

Acts 20:37 *They wept aloud as they embraced*
him in farewell.
Express your emotions to trusted friends, your
pastor, or a counselor. Sometimes God will
provide comfort through the words and help
of other believers.

How does God use people's broken hearts?

Joel 2:13 *Don't tear your clothing in your grief;*
instead, tear your hearts. Return to the Lord your

God, for he is gracious and merciful. He is not easily angered. He is filled with kindness and is eager not to punish you.

Our broken hearts can lead us to God. Humility is a good starting place on the road to God because it puts God and our problems in proper perspective.

James 4:9 *Let there be tears for the wrong things you have done. Let there be sorrow and deep grief. Let there be sadness instead of laughter, and gloom instead of joy.*

Psalm 51:17 *The sacrifice you want is a broken spirit. A broken and repentant heart, O God, you will not despise.*

2 Corinthians 7:9 *Now I am glad I sent it, not because it hurt you, but because the pain caused you to have remorse and change your ways.*

Our broken hearts can lead us to a realization, confession, and repentance of sin. When our hearts break, they sometimes reveal the sin within and the need for the Lord to wash that sin away.

Psalm 30:11 *You have turned my mourning into joyful dancing. You have taken away my clothes of mourning and clothed me with joy.*

Brokenness leads to healing, and healing leads to rejoicing.

2 Corinthians 1:6 *So when we are weighed down with troubles, it is for your benefit and salvation!*

For when God comforts us, it is so that we, in turn, can be an encouragement to you. Then you can patiently endure the same things we suffer.
Our broken hearts can help us comfort others. In our brokenness, we understand others who are broken.

How can I help brokenhearted people?

Psalm 69:20 *Their insults have broken my heart, and I am in despair. If only one person would show some pity; if only one would turn and comfort me.*
You can give your attention, empathy, and comfort to the brokenhearted. Insults and cruel words are abrasive, wounding the heart. Attention, empathy, and comfort are therapeutic, healing the heart.

Proverbs 15:13 *A glad heart makes a happy face; a broken heart crushes the spirit.*

Proverbs 17:22 *A cheerful heart is good medicine, but a broken spirit saps a person's strength.*
You can be aware of the effects of being brokenhearted on a person's spirit, mind, and body. Awareness leads to sympathy; sympathy leads to empathy; empathy leads to helping the wounded, and that leads to a time of healing.

Romans 12:15 *When others are happy, be happy with them. If they are sad, share their sorrow.*
You can share in others' sorrow as surely as you can share in their joy.

2 Corinthians 1:4 *He comforts us in all our troubles so that we can comfort others. When others are troubled, we will be able to give them the same comfort God has given us.*

You can share your experiences of God's comfort. In the pattern of God's healing, others may find healing in you. In bringing comfort, you are comforted.

Job 21:34 *How can you comfort me? All your explanations are wrong!*

Job 16:2 *I have heard all this before. What miserable comforters you are!*

You need to be careful with the words you use to the brokenhearted. Explanations and clichés are rarely comforting. Love, sympathy, and the power of your presence are urgently needed. Sometimes the best comfort you can give is just to be there.

1 Thessalonians 3:7 *So we have been greatly comforted, dear friends, in all of our own crushing troubles and suffering, because you have remained strong in your faith.*

You can remain strong in your own faith. Those weakened by hurt are encouraged to see others who have overcome similar hurt.

Job 42:11 *Then all his brothers, sisters, and former friends came and feasted with him in his home. And they consoled him and comforted him because of all the trials the Lord had brought against*

him. And each of them brought him a gift of money
and a gold ring.

Psalm 68:6 *God places the lonely in families;
he sets the prisoners free and gives them joy.*

PROMISES FROM GOD: Psalm
34:18 *The Lord is close to the brokenhearted; he
rescues those who are crushed in spirit.*

Psalm 40:2 *He lifted me out of the pit of despair,
out of the mud and the mire. He set my feet on solid
ground and steadied me as I walked along.*

Building Others Up

(*see also* ENCOURAGEMENT)

What can we do to build each other up?
Proverbs 15:30 *A cheerful look brings joy to the
heart; good news makes for good health.*
We can build one another up simply by means
of a look that communicates approval and
acceptance.

Hebrews 10:24 *Think of ways to encourage one
another to outbursts of love and good deeds.*
We can build one another up by regular, inten-
tional encouragement.

2 Corinthians 13:11 *Dear friends, I close
my letter with these last words: Rejoice. Change*

your ways. Encourage each other. Live in harmony and peace. Then the God of love and peace will be with you.

1 Thessalonians 5:11 *So encourage each other and build each other up, just as you are already doing.*

Ephesians 4:29 *Don't use foul or abusive language. Let everything you say be good and helpful, so that your words will be an encouragement to those who hear them.*
We can build one another up by living in harmony and peace.

1 Samuel 23:16 *Jonathan went to find David and encouraged him to stay strong in his faith in God.*

Acts 11:23 *When he arrived and saw this proof of God's favor, he was filled with joy, and he encouraged the believers to stay true to the Lord.*
We can build one another up by encouraging each other's relationship with God.

Titus 1:9 *He must have a strong and steadfast belief in the trustworthy message he was taught; then he will be able to encourage others with right teaching and show those who oppose it where they are wrong.*
We can build one another up by sharing God's Word of instruction and by worshiping God together.

Romans 12:10 *Love each other with genuine affection, and take delight in honoring each other.* We can build one another up by showing each other honor and respect.

Romans 15:2 *We should please others. If we do what helps them, we will build them up in the Lord.* We can build one another up by cultivating an attitude that puts others first.

PROMISE FROM GOD: 2 Corinthians 13:11 *Dear friends, I close my letter with these last words: Rejoice. Change your ways. Encourage each other. Live in harmony and peace. Then the God of love and peace will be with you.*

Burnout

How do I know if I am experiencing burnout?

2 Samuel 21:15 *When David and his men were in the thick of battle, David became weak and exhausted.*

Psalm 38:8 *I am exhausted and completely crushed. My groans come from an anguished heart.* If you become weak and exhausted in the middle of doing your work, you may be experiencing burnout.

1 Kings 19:14 *I alone am left, and now they are trying to kill me, too.*

You may be experiencing burnout if you despair because your work seems fruitless.

Psalm 69:1-2 *The floodwaters are up to my neck. Deeper and deeper I sink into the mire; I can't find a foothold to stand on.*
It may be burnout if you feel overwhelmed by everything that is going on in your life.

Jeremiah 45:3 *You have said, "I am overwhelmed with trouble! Haven't I had enough pain already? And now the Lord has added more!"*
When you become burned out, you may feel bitter toward God.

What is the antidote for burnout?
Exodus 18:21-23 *Find some capable, honest men. . . . They will help you carry the load, making the task easier for you. If you follow this advice, . . . then you will be able to endure the pressures.*
See if you can delegate some of your workload.

Exodus 23:12 *Work for six days, and rest on the seventh. . . . It will also allow the people of your household . . . to be refreshed.*
Make sure that you get regular, consistent rest. This is an important part of avoiding and recovering from burnout.

1 Kings 19:5-8 *As he was sleeping, an angel touched him and told him, "Get up and eat!". . . So he ate and drank and lay down again. Then the angel*

of the Lord came again and touched him and said, "Get up and eat some more, for there is a long journey ahead of you." So he got up and ate and drank.
Take good care of your body, including exercising, resting, and eating nutritious meals. These activities will help you overcome burnout. Poor nutrition or health habits invite burnout.

Nehemiah 6:9 *So I prayed for strength to continue the work.*

2 Thessalonians 2:16-17 *May our Lord Jesus Christ and God our Father . . . comfort your hearts and give you strength in every good thing you do and say.*
Sometimes you can't stop working, even though you feel exhausted. When you need to finish a job, you can pray to God for strength to keep going until you reach a stopping place or until the job is completed. If you're working with other people, encourage each other to persevere.

Matthew 11:28-29 *Come to me, all of you who are weary and carry heavy burdens, and I will give you rest . . . and you will find rest for your souls.*
It is crucial to renew your fellowship with God and be restored by spending time with him. Connecting with God taps into his strength.

PROMISE FROM GOD: Isaiah 40:29-31 *He gives power to those who are tired and worn out; he offers strength to the weak. Even*

44

youths will become exhausted, and young men will give up. But those who wait on the Lord will find new strength. They will fly high on wings like eagles. They will run and not grow weary. They will walk and not faint.

Busyness

What are the benefits of being busy?

Ecclesiastes 11:6 *Be sure to stay busy and plant a variety of crops, for you never know which will grow—perhaps they all will.*

Rich harvests cannot come from lazy fingers. If we want fruitfulness in any facet of our lives, we must get busy now.

What are the dangers of too much busyness?

Proverbs 19:2 *Zeal without knowledge is not good; a person who moves too quickly may go the wrong way.*

Psalm 39:6 *We are merely moving shadows, and all our busy rushing ends in nothing. We heap up wealth for someone else to spend.*

Never confuse activity with accomplishment. A too-full schedule may reflect a lack of wise priorities. Activity without God will always come up empty-handed.

How can I find rest from the busyness of life?

Exodus 34:21 *Six days are set aside for work, but on the Sabbath day you must rest, even during the seasons of plowing and harvest.*

Psalm 91:1 *Those who live in the shelter of the Most High will find rest in the shadow of the Almighty.*
God is both the model and the source of rest. As God rested after creation was finished, so he provides and encourages rest from your labors.

Mark 6:31 *Then Jesus said, "Let's get away from the crowds for a while and rest." There were so many people coming and going that Jesus and his disciples didn't even have time to eat.*
You need to prioritize time for rest and renewal rather than letting the demands of others completely dictate your schedule. God planned for work, but he also planned for rest. Keep both in balance.

How can I be less busy?

Mark 1:36-38 *Later Simon and the others went to find him. They said, "Everyone is asking for you." But he replied, "We must go on to other towns as well, and I will preach to them too, because that is why I came."*
Freeing yourself from the trap of incessant activity requires learning to say no—even to worthwhile activities.

PROMISE FROM GOD: Matthew 11:28-29 *Then Jesus said, "Come to me, all of you who are weary and carry heavy burdens, and I will give you rest. Take my yoke upon you. Let me teach you, because I am humble and gentle, and you will find rest for your souls."*

Celebration

Regardless of my personal circumstances, what can I always celebrate?

Isaiah 49:13 *Sing for joy, O heavens! Rejoice, O earth! Burst into song, O mountains! For the Lord has comforted his people and will have compassion on them in their sorrow.*

Sometimes you can celebrate the joy of good circumstances, but always you can celebrate the Lord himself!

What kinds of things can spark celebration?

Deuteronomy 16:14-15 *This festival will be a happy time of rejoicing with your family . . . to honor the Lord, . . . for it is [he] who gives you bountiful harvests and blesses all your work.*
We celebrate to thank God for all he has done for us, to recall his acts of goodness, and to enjoy each other's company.

47

Exodus 13:4-5, 8 *This day in early spring will be the anniversary of your exodus. You must celebrate this day. . . . During these festival days each year, you must explain to your children why you are celebrating.*
We celebrate to mark important milestones in our lives. We also celebrate to teach our children the ultimate reason for our celebration.

Psalm 98:4, 6 *Shout to the Lord, all the earth; break out in praise and sing for joy! . . . Make a joyful symphony before the Lord, the King!*
We celebrate to praise and worship God because of who he is, because he loves us, because of the blessings he has given us on earth, and because of the eternal blessings he has waiting for us in heaven.

What are the ingredients of celebration?
Nehemiah 8:10 *Go and celebrate with a feast, . . . and share gifts of food with people who have nothing prepared. This is a sacred day. . . . Don't be dejected and sad, for the joy of the Lord is your strength!*
Joy, fun, food, and feasting—as God intended— are important parts of celebration because they lift our spirits and help us see the beauty and meaning in life.

Leviticus 23:25 *You must do no regular work on that day.*
Celebration requires taking time out of our

normal routines. Celebration allows us to rest and focus on what is good, taking our minds off the mundane and the ordinary.

1 Chronicles 13:8 *David and all Israel were celebrating before God with all their might, singing and playing all kinds of musical instruments—lyres, harps, tambourines, cymbals, and trumpets.* Celebration brings out our energy, enthusiasm, and joy, ultimately focusing them on the praise of God.

PROMISE FROM GOD: Psalm 5:11 *But let all who take refuge in you rejoice; let them sing joyful praises forever. Protect them, so all who love your name may be filled with joy.*

Chaos

(*see also* BUSYNESS)

How can I restore order in my sometimes chaotic life?

John 16:33 *I have told you all this so that you may have peace in me. Here on earth you will have many trials and sorrows. But take heart, because I have overcome the world.*
Regardless of your circumstances, your hope and peace are grounded in Jesus. Knowing your future brings order of priorities and security to your life.

Romans 15:5 *May God, who gives this patience and encouragement, help you live in complete harmony with each other—each with the attitude of Christ Jesus toward the other.*
You can restore harmony to your relationships by modeling Jesus' attitude toward relationships.

How do I restore order to my inner spirit?

Proverbs 15:16 *It is better to have little with fear for the Lord than to have great treasure with turmoil.*

Psalm 61:2 *From the ends of the earth, I will cry to you for help, for my heart is overwhelmed. Lead me to the towering rock of safety.*
Pursue knowing the Lord God, the Creator of order and peace.

Romans 5:1 *Therefore, since we have been made right in God's sight by faith, we have peace with God because of what Jesus Christ our Lord has done for us.*
God is constantly at work to give you inner peace as you follow him. Don't prevent his work in your heart and mind.

Romans 16:17 *And now I make one more appeal, my dear brothers and sisters. Watch out for people who cause divisions and upset people's faith by teaching things that are contrary to what you have been taught. Stay away from them.*
Guard what you hear and believe; watch the company that you keep. Chaos is often the result

of not being diligent in avoiding that which causes strife and division in your life. Guard carefully the gates to your soul because chaos, like an enemy army, will invade and disrupt your peace with God.

PROMISES FROM GOD: Isaiah 45:18 *For the Lord is God, and he created the heavens and earth and put everything in place. He made the world to be lived in, not to be a place of empty chaos. "I am the Lord," he says, "and there is no other."*

1 Corinthians 14:33 *For God is not a God of disorder but of peace, as in all the other churches.*

Circumstances

Is God in control of my circumstances?

Psalm 135:6 *The Lord does whatever pleases him throughout all heaven and earth, and on the seas and in their depths.*

Isaiah 45:7 *I am the one who creates the light and makes the darkness. I am the one who sends good times and bad times. I, the Lord, am the one who does these things.*

James 4:13-15 *Look here, you people who say, "Today or tomorrow we are going to a certain town and will stay there a year. We will do business there*

*and make a profit." How do you know what will
happen tomorrow? For your life is like the morning
fog—it's here a little while, then it's gone. What you
ought to say is, "If the Lord wants us to, we will live
and do this or that."*

Not only is God in control of life circumstances,
but he is able to bring good out of any circumstance.

How does God view my circumstances?
How should I view my circumstances?

2 Chronicles 32:7-8 *"Be strong and courageous! Don't be afraid of the king of Assyria or his
mighty army, for there is a power far greater on our
side! He may have a great army, but they are just
men. We have the Lord our God to help us and to
fight our battles for us!" These words greatly encouraged the people.*

Psalm 34:1 *I will praise the Lord at all times.
I will constantly speak his praises.*

Because you know God, you can view life circumstances with his perspective. Try to understand
his ways, his thoughts, his view of your situation.
The more you walk in godliness, the more you
will see things the way God sees them. The more
you avoid godliness, the more you see only your
own ways.

Isaiah 45:9 *Destruction is certain for those
who argue with their Creator. Does a clay pot ever*

argue with its maker? Does the clay dispute with the one who shapes it, saying, "Stop, you are doing it wrong!" Does the pot exclaim, "How clumsy can you be!"

Romans 8:28 *And we know that God causes everything to work together for the good of those who love God and are called according to his purpose for them.*

View life circumstances through the lens of God's design, control, and authority. Did you create the universe? Who did? Did you create your own life? Who did? Can you fully comprehend yourself and your own circumstances? Who can? Only God. Why then would you not want to entrust yourself to him?

Hebrews 11:11 *It was by faith that Sarah together with Abraham was able to have a child, even though they were too old and Sarah was barren. Abraham believed that God would keep his promise.*

View God working in life circumstances through eyes and hearts of faith. The "glasses" you wear color the view.

How should I respond to life circumstances?

Habakkuk 3:17-19 *Even though the fig trees have no blossoms, and there are no grapes on the vine; even though the olive crop fails, and the fields lie empty and barren; even though the flocks die in the fields, and the cattle barns are empty, yet I will* *rejoice in the Lord! I will be joyful in the God of my salvation. The Sovereign Lord is my strength! He will make me as surefooted as a deer and bring me safely over the mountains.*

Focus more on the joy, peace, and future that come from a relationship with God and less on your daily circumstances. You can always respond joyfully to the God who offers you the eternal gift of salvation. The more you wallow in unpleasant circumstances, the more they may drag you under. The more you reach out to God, the more he can lift you up.

Ecclesiastes 7:14 *Enjoy prosperity while you can. But when hard times strike, realize that both come from God. That way you will realize that nothing is certain in this life.*

1 Thessalonians 5:18 *No matter what happens, always be thankful, for this is God's will for you who belong to Christ Jesus.*

Accept life's circumstances with thanksgiving to God, as well as trust in him for his constant presence and comfort. Whether you are currently living in sunshine or rain, God never changes and his love for you never changes. God is always eager to teach you something from both the good and the bad.

Philippians 4:6 *Don't worry about anything; instead, pray about everything. Tell God what you need, and thank him for all he has done.*

Refuse to worry. One of the hardest lessons of life is to turn worry into confident prayer when bad circumstances come your way. Come to God with your needs in thanksgiving for what he has done for you, trusting that he will bring good out of the difficult.

Jeremiah 42:6 *Whether we like it or not, we will obey the Lord our God to whom we send you with our plea. For if we obey him, everything will turn out well for us.*

Respond in obedience to God in every circumstance. He sees the larger picture and the future.

Romans 8:37-39 *No, despite all these things, overwhelming victory is ours through Christ, who loved us. And I am convinced that nothing can ever separate us from his love. Death can't, and life can't. The angels can't, and the demons can't. Our fears for today, our worries about tomorrow, and even the powers of hell can't keep God's love away. Whether we are high above the sky or in the deepest ocean, nothing in all creation will ever be able to separate us from the love of God that is revealed in Christ Jesus our Lord.*

Respond with confidence in God's love for you. When times are tough, you may blame God and think he doesn't love you. But that is when you need his love the most.

How can I make the most of my circumstances?

Jeremiah 17:7-8 *But blessed are those who trust in the Lord and have made the Lord their hope and confidence. They are like trees planted along a riverbank, with roots that reach deep into the water. Such trees are not bothered by the heat or worried by long months of drought. Their leaves stay green, and they go right on producing delicious fruit.*

Trust in the Lord; he is worthy of your hope and confidence. Those who trust in the Lord understand the secret of his life-sustaining power.

Esther 4:13-14 *Mordecai sent back this reply to Esther: "Don't think for a moment that you will escape there in the palace when all other Jews are killed. If you keep quiet at a time like this, deliverance for the Jews will arise from some other place, but you and your relatives will die. What's more, who can say but that you have been elevated to the palace for just such a time as this?"*

God can use you as you are. Start with who you are and what you have, not with who you wish you were and what you don't have.

James 1:2-3 *Dear brothers and sisters, whenever trouble comes your way, let it be an opportunity for joy. For when your faith is tested, your endurance has a chance to grow.*

You can experience joy and growth in difficult circumstances. Plants continue to grow even on

56

cloudy days. Life can continue to flourish despite cloudy circumstances.

How does God use circumstances for good?

Romans 5:3 *We can rejoice, too, when we run into problems and trials, for we know that they are good for us—they help us learn to endure.*

1 Peter 1:5-7 *And God, in his mighty power, will protect you until you receive this salvation, because you are trusting him. It will be revealed on the last day for all to see. So be truly glad! There is wonderful joy ahead, even though it is necessary for you to endure many trials for a while. These trials are only to test your faith, to show that it is strong and pure.*
God uses our circumstances for our own personal growth—for our good. We don't always know why God sometimes allows bad circumstances to come our way, but we do know that God always wants to bring good out of the bad.

Philippians 1:12-14 *And I want you to know, dear friends, that everything that has happened to me here has helped to spread the Good News. For everyone here, including all the soldiers in the palace guard, knows that I am in chains because of Christ. And because of my imprisonment, many of the Christians here have gained confidence and become more bold in telling others about Christ.*
God uses our circumstances to help us grow. Then we can help others grow. Anyone can be

joyful and faithful when life is going well, but when life gets tough believers have a unique opportunity to show how a relationship with God brings comfort, confidence, and hope—to us and to others.

How can I see God when things look bad?

Nehemiah 6:16 *When our enemies and the surrounding nations heard about it, they were frightened and humiliated. They realized that this work had been done with the help of our God.*

John 11:21-22, 32 *Martha said to Jesus, "Lord, if you had been here, my brother would not have died. But even now I know that God will give you whatever you ask."... When Mary arrived and saw Jesus, she fell down at his feet and said, "Lord, if you had been here, my brother would not have died."*
If God went to such great trouble to create us and a world for us to live in, to send his Son to die for our sins, and to prepare an eternal home for us in heaven, why would he abandon us in our day-to-day circumstances? Watch closely for God's presence and his power in yesterday, today, and tomorrow. Pray for his intervention in your life, and then watch for those answers to prayer.

PROMISE FROM GOD:
Psalm 112:4, 6-8 *When darkness overtakes the godly, light will come bursting in. They are generous, compassionate, and righteous. . . . Such people will*

not be overcome by evil circumstances. Those who are righteous will be long remembered. They do not fear bad news; they confidently trust the Lord to care for them. They are confident and fearless and can face their foes triumphantly.

Community

Why do I need fellowship with other Christians?

Acts 14:22 *They strengthened the believers. They encouraged them to continue in the faith, reminding them that they must enter into the Kingdom of God through many tribulations.*

Acts 18:23 *Paul went back to Galatia and Phrygia, visiting all the believers, encouraging them and helping them to grow in the Lord.*
You need their encouragement. When you are down, you need others to lift you up.

Luke 17:3 *I am warning you! If another believer sins, rebuke him; then if he repents, forgive him.*

1 Corinthians 5:12 *It isn't my responsibility to judge outsiders, but it certainly is your job to judge those inside the church who are sinning in these ways.*
You need their accountability. When you are headed in the wrong direction, you need others to help you go the right way.

Acts 2:44 *And all the believers met together constantly and shared everything they had.*
You need their generosity in times of need. When you have less, they will provide. When you have more, you can share.

Acts 12:5 *While Peter was in prison, the church prayed very earnestly for him.*
You need their prayers. When you are in trouble, you need others to ask God to help you.

What are the characteristics of authentic Christian community?

Acts 9:31 *The church then had peace throughout Judea, Galilee, and Samaria, and it grew in strength and numbers. The believers were walking in the fear of the Lord and in the comfort of the Holy Spirit.*

1 Corinthians 12:5 *There are different kinds of service in the church, but it is the same Lord we are serving.*
We find comfort and gain strength from other believers who reach out in love and peace. There is special power when we love, respect, and worship God together.

Matthew 21:13 *The Scriptures declare, "My Temple will be called a place of prayer."*

Acts 12:5, 12 *While Peter was in prison, the church prayed very earnestly for him. . . . After a little*

thought, he went to the home of Mary, the mother of John Mark, where many were gathered for prayer.
We learn to pray together. There is special power in the prayers of believers gathered together.

Psalm 26:12 *I have taken a stand, and I will publicly praise the Lord.*

Psalm 35:18 *Then I will thank you in front of the entire congregation. I will praise you before all the people.*

Hebrews 2:12 *For he said to God, "I will declare the wonder of your name to my brothers and sisters. I will praise you among all your people."*
We praise God together. There is special power in our united praise.

Acts 19:18 *Many who became believers confessed their sinful practices.*

Ezra 9:5-6, 15 *At the time of the sacrifice, I stood up from where I had sat in mourning with my clothes torn. . . . I prayed, "O my God, I am utterly ashamed; I blush to lift up my face to you. For our sins are piled higher than our heads, and our guilt has reached to the heavens. . . . O Lord, God of Israel, you are just. We stand before you in our guilt as nothing but an escaped remnant, though in such a condition none of us can stand in your presence."*
We mutually support one another in dealing with our sins and problems. At times we must confess our sins corporately as a means to keep us

accountable to right living. There is special power
in mutual support.

Nehemiah 8:1, 3 *All the people assembled
together as one person at the square just inside the
Water Gate. They asked Ezra the scribe to bring out
the Book of the Law of Moses. . . . He faced the
square just inside the Water Gate from early morning
until noon and read aloud to everyone who could
understand.*
We delight in reading and hearing God's Word
together. There is special power in sharing God's
Word together.

Acts 2:42, 46-47 *They joined with the other
believers and devoted themselves to the apostles'
teaching and fellowship, sharing in the Lord's Supper
and in prayer. . . . They worshiped together at the
Temple each day, met in homes for the Lord's Supper,
and shared their meals with great joy and generosity—all the while praising God and enjoying the
goodwill of all the people. And each day the Lord
added to their group those who were being saved.*
We study God's Word together, we fellowship
together, we share in the Lord's Supper together,
and we pray together. We experience spiritual
growth together as God adds to his church. There
is special power in doing godly activities together.

1 John 1:7 *But if we are living in the light of
God's presence, just as Christ is, then we have fellow-*

ship with each other, and the blood of Jesus, his Son, cleanses us from every sin.

Psalm 55:14 *What good fellowship we enjoyed as we walked together to the house of God.*
We have wonderful fellowship with each other and God. There is special power in uniting as one in the Lord.

Galatians 6:2 *Share each other's troubles and problems, and in this way obey the law of Christ.*
We share each other's difficulties in life and mutually support one another. There is special power in lifting each other up.

How can we best impact our communities?

Galatians 5:14 *For the whole law can be summed up in this one command: "Love your neighbor as yourself."*

Romans 13:8 *Pay all your debts, except the debt of love for others. You can never finish paying that! If you love your neighbor, you will fulfill all the requirements of God's law.*
We are to love those God has placed in our lives.

1 Peter 2:12 *Be careful how you live among your unbelieving neighbors. Even if they accuse you of doing wrong, they will see your honorable behavior, and they will believe and give honor to God when he comes to judge the world.*
We are to live honorably among our neighbors.

1 Peter 3:15-16 *If you are asked about your Christian hope, always be ready to explain it. But you must do this in a gentle and respectful way. Keep your conscience clear.*

We are to be prepared to tell everyone of our hope in Christ with gentleness and respect. Our lives should confirm our message.

2 Peter 2:5 *Noah warned the world of God's righteous judgment.*

Acts 9:36 *There was a believer in Joppa named Tabitha. . . . She was always doing kind things for others and helping the poor.*

We are to be willing to be used in whatever way God desires in our community—whether it be to warn others of sin, serve our neighbors, declare his work in our own lives, show hospitality, or reach out to the needy.

What makes a community of believers?

Ephesians 3:6 *And this is the secret plan: The Gentiles have an equal share with the Jews in all the riches inherited by God's children. Both groups have believed the Good News, and both are part of the same body and enjoy together the promise of blessings through Christ Jesus.*

A community of believers believes the Good News of Christ Jesus.

Deuteronomy 7:6 *For you are a holy people, who belong to the Lord your God.*

1 Corinthians 1:2 *We are writing to the church of God in Corinth, you who have been called by God to be his own holy people. He made you holy by means of Christ Jesus, just as he did all Christians everywhere—whoever calls upon the name of Jesus Christ, our Lord and theirs.*

A community of believers has been chosen by God to be his holy people.

1 Corinthians 3:23 *You belong to Christ, and Christ belongs to God.*

John 17:9-10 *My prayer is not for the world, but for those you have given me, because they belong to you. And all of them, since they are mine, belong to you; and you have given them back to me, so they are my glory!*

Romans 1:6 *You are among those who have been called to belong to Jesus Christ.*

A community of believers is made up of those who belong to the Lord.

1 Corinthians 12:13 *Some of us are Jews, some are Gentiles, some are slaves, and some are free. But we have all been baptized into Christ's body by one Spirit, and we have all received the same Spirit.*

A community of believers has the same spirit and the same eternity ahead.

1 John 4:19 *We love each other as a result of his loving us first.*

1 Peter 1:22 *Now you can have sincere love for each other as brothers and sisters because you were cleansed from your sins when you accepted the truth of the Good News. So see to it that you really do love each other intensely with all your hearts.*

John 15:12 *I command you to love each other in the same way that I love you.*

Romans 12:10 *Love each other with genuine affection, and take delight in honoring each other.*
A community of believers loves one another.

Deuteronomy 7:12 *If you listen to these regulations and obey them faithfully, the Lord your God will keep his covenant of unfailing love with you.*
A community of believers keeps each other accountable to obey God.

1 Corinthians 12:12, 14, 19-20 *The human body has many parts, but the many parts make up only one body. So it is with the body of Christ. . . . Yes, the body has many different parts, not just one part. . . . What a strange thing a body would be if it had only one part! Yes, there are many parts, but only one body.*
A community of believers is made up of individuals who each make a unique contribution to the one body in Christ.

1 Corinthians 1:10 *Now, dear brothers and sisters, I appeal to you by the authority of the Lord Jesus Christ to stop arguing among yourselves. Let*

there be real harmony so there won't be divisions in the church. I plead with you to be of one mind, united in thought and purpose.

1 Peter 3:8 *Finally, all of you should be of one mind, full of sympathy toward each other, loving one another with tender hearts and humble minds.*

Psalm 133:1 *How wonderful it is, how pleasant, when brothers live together in harmony!*
A community of believers, though made up of many people, finds a way to be unified in thought and purpose. There is harmony with one another.

Romans 12:5 *We are all parts of his one body, and each of us has different work to do. And since we are all one body in Christ, we belong to each other, and each of us needs all the others.*
A community of believers depends on one another.

PROMISES FROM GOD:
Deuteronomy 28:9 *If you obey the commands of the Lord your God and walk in his ways, the Lord will establish you as his holy people as he solemnly promised to do.*

Matthew 18:20 *For where two or three gather together because they are mine, I am there among them.*

Condemnation

(*see also* ACCUSATIONS)

Will God condemn me for my sins?

Isaiah 26:21 *The Lord is coming from heaven to punish the people of the earth for their sins.*
Judgment and punishment are promised for all sin.

Romans 3:25 *For God sent Jesus to take the punishment for our sins. . . . We are made right with God when we believe that Jesus shed his blood, sacrificing his life for us.*
If you have put your faith in Jesus and so belong to him, you have been freed forever from condemnation. You will not be condemned because you recognize and accept that Jesus bore the ultimate punishment for your sins—death—when he died in your place. He declares you "not guilty."

How can I experience this freedom from condemnation?

John 3:16-17 *For God so loved the world that he gave his only Son, so that everyone who believes in him will not perish but have eternal life. God did not send his Son into the world to condemn it, but to save it.*
You escape God's condemnation when you accept God's love by believing in Jesus Christ as

Savior. When you realize that he died for your sins so you wouldn't have to, you understand his great love for you, which allows your love for him to begin to grow. You then begin a lifelong journey of getting to know him and experiencing his love for you.

R o m a n s 3 : 2 4 *Yet now God in his gracious kindness declares us not guilty. He has done this through Christ Jesus, who has freed us by taking away our sins.*

T i t u s 3 : 7 *He declared us not guilty because of his great kindness. And now we know that we will inherit eternal life.*

You escape God's condemnation when you accept God's kindness. Although you deserve judgment for sin, you instead experience daily grace and eternal blessings from God.

J o h n 5 : 2 4 *I assure you, those who listen to my message and believe in God who sent me have eternal life. They will never be condemned for their sins, but they have already passed from death into life.*

You escape God's condemnation when you believe in God and accept his pardoning gift of eternal life. There is no greater gift than eternal life with God and fellow believers in heaven.

How can I change my own condemning attitude?

2 C o r i n t h i a n s 5 : 1 7 *What this means is that those who become Christians become new persons.*

They are not the same anymore, for the old life is gone. A new life has begun!
God can give you a fresh start when you come to him—*he* can change your heart.

Psalm 139:23-24 *Search me, O God, and know my heart; test me and know my thoughts. Point out anything in me that offends you, and lead me along the path of everlasting life.*
Ask him to examine your life. Respond to his findings and follow his ways.

Romans 14:10, 13 *So why do you condemn another Christian? Why do you look down on another Christian? Remember, each of us will stand personally before the judgment seat of God. . . . So don't condemn each other anymore. Decide instead to live in such a way that you will not put an obstacle in another Christian's path.*
Each of us will stand alone before God for him to judge us. So why are we trying to do his work of judging others? Seek to live your life helping others follow God instead of condemning others when they stumble.

PROMISE FROM GOD: Romans 8:31, 33-34 *What can we say about such wonderful things as these? If God is for us, who can ever be against us? . . . Who dares accuse us whom God has chosen for his own? Will God? No! He is the one who has given us right standing with himself.*

Who then will condemn us? Will Christ Jesus? No,
for he is the one who died for us and was raised to life
for us and is sitting at the place of highest honor next
to God, pleading for us.

Confidence

(*see also* FAITH or HOPE or TRUST)

Where do I get my confidence?

Psalm 118:8 *It is better to trust the Lord than*
to put confidence in people.
Confidence comes from knowing that God is
completely trustworthy and that he will always
do what he says.

Psalm 27:1 *The Lord is my light and my salva-*
tion—so why should I be afraid?
Confidence comes from knowing with certainty
that you are saved and that an eternal home
awaits you. You no longer need to fear anything
because your life is secure in him.

John 14:1-3 *Don't be troubled. . . . I am going*
to prepare a place for you. . . . When everything is
ready, I will come and get you.
Jesus' promises and preparations can give you
confidence about your eternal future.

What if I've lost my confidence in others, especially those who have broken a trust?

Proverbs 25:19 *Putting confidence in an unreliable person is like chewing with a toothache or walking on a broken foot.*
It is important to love others and give them the benefit of the doubt. But it is foolish to depend on someone who has a record of failed trust.

What happens when I lose confidence in God?

Job 23:3 *If only I knew where to find God, I would go to his throne and talk with him there.*
When tragedy strikes, your first inclination may be to wonder what happened to God. Nagging doubts cause you to question his care for you. But God's love and care are endless. Go to him, talk to him, tell him your fears. He will answer and give you the comfort that you need.

Matthew 11:28 *Come to me, all of you who are weary and carry heavy burdens, and I will give you rest.*
When you begin to doubt God, run *to* him not *away* from him. How else will you discover how much he really loves you?

What's the difference between healthy confidence and unhealthy pride?

1 John 3:2 *But we do know that when he comes we will be like him.*
Healthy confidence is a realization and an assurance that God loves you, that he has given you

talents and gifts, that he wants you to use those gifts for him, and that he has given you salvation and eternal life in heaven. Knowing this gives you complete certainty that your life can have meaning now and forever.

2 Chronicles 26:16 *When he had become powerful, he also became proud, which led to his downfall.*
Unhealthy pride, as opposed to healthy confidence, is the ingredient that causes confidence to become arrogant and cocky. If you think you can do it yourself, or you stop seeking God's help, these are the warning signs that confidence has turned to arrogance.

PROMISE FROM GOD: Jeremiah 17:7 *But blessed are those who trust in the Lord and have made the Lord their hope and confidence.*

Confusion

How should I deal with life's confusion?
Psalm 94:19 *When doubts filled my mind, your comfort gave me renewed hope and cheer.*
As you focus your time and thoughts on God, it becomes clear what he wants you to do. The confusion doesn't seem so great because he is the God of order and peace. Life is less confusing

when you realize he truly is in control. How wonderful to know that when you are confused, God has an answer. Just ask.

Psalm 75:3 *When the earth quakes and its people live in turmoil, I am the one who keeps its foundations firm.*

Isaiah 45:18 *For the Lord is God, and he created the heavens and earth and put everything in place. He made the world to be lived in, not to be a place of empty chaos. "I am the Lord," he says, "and there is no other."*

The world can be a pretty confusing place. As a believer, you can trust God and recognize his sovereignty. With the help of a sovereign God, confusion seems manageable. You know that one day God will take away all the confusion and bring his kingdom of peace.

Proverbs 20:24 *How can we understand the road we travel? It is the Lord who directs our steps.*

James 1:5 *If you need wisdom—if you want to know what God wants you to do—ask him, and he will gladly tell you. He will not resent your asking.* Seeing life through your limited vision brings confusion and frustration. Ask God for understanding. His wisdom will help you sort out the confusion.

2 Timothy 3:16 *All Scripture is inspired by God and is useful to teach us what is true and to make us*

realize what is wrong in our lives. It straightens us out and teaches us to do what is right.

Look to Scripture for instruction and understanding. God will give you wisdom to deal with any situation. Through the Word of God you discover the mind of God.

John 16:13 *When the Spirit of truth comes, he will guide you into all truth. He will not be presenting his own ideas; he will be telling you what he has heard. He will tell you about the future.*

1 Corinthians 2:9-10, 13 *That is what the Scriptures mean when they say, "No eye has seen, no ear has heard, and no mind has imagined what God has prepared for those who love him." But we know these things because God has revealed them to us by his Spirit, and his Spirit searches out everything and shows us even God's deep secrets. . . . When we tell you this, we do not use words of human wisdom. We speak words given to us by the Spirit, using the Spirit's words to explain spiritual truths.*

Be sensitive to the Holy Spirit. He gives the power to deal with confusion. Since you don't know the mysteries of life, you need the One who understands and knows all things to guide you.

2 Timothy 4:2-3 *Preach the word of God. Be persistent, whether the time is favorable or not. Patiently correct, rebuke, and encourage your people with good teaching. For a time is coming when people*

will no longer listen to right teaching. They will follow their own desires and will look for teachers who will tell them whatever they want to hear.

Hebrews 13:17 *Obey your spiritual leaders and do what they say. Their work is to watch over your souls, and they know they are accountable to God. Give them reason to do this joyfully and not with sorrow. That would certainly not be for your benefit. Listen to wise teaching. You will learn what to do.*

Ephesians 4:14 *Then we will no longer be like children, forever changing our minds about what we believe because someone has told us something different or because someone has cleverly lied to us and made the lie sound like the truth.*

Philippians 1:9-10 *I pray that your love for each other will overflow more and more, and that you will keep on growing in your knowledge and understanding. For I want you to understand what really matters, so that you may live pure and blameless lives until Christ returns.*

When you refuse to give up and quit, you continue to grow toward spiritual maturity. As you mature in Christ, you can learn to better handle the confusing things of life.

How can I avoid confusion?

Proverbs 3:5-6 *Trust in the Lord with all your heart; do not depend on your own understanding. Seek his will in all you do, and he will direct your paths.*

Be a devoted follower of God—constantly and deliberately deciding to trust him and follow his Word, which gives you focus and purpose.

How should I respond when I don't understand God?

Hebrews 10:23 Without wavering, let us hold tightly to the hope we say we have, for God can be trusted to keep his promise.

Trust God and trust that what he says in his Word is true. If that is your compass for direction in life, you will always know what to do and which way to go. It is when you doubt God that life gets confusing.

Acts 10:19 Meanwhile, as Peter was puzzling over the vision, the Holy Spirit said to him, "Three men have come looking for you."

Be sensitive to the Holy Spirit.

Jonah 4:1-4 This change of plans upset Jonah, and he became very angry. So he complained to the Lord about it: "Didn't I say before I left home that you would do this, Lord? That is why I ran away to Tarshish! I knew that you were a gracious and compassionate God, slow to get angry and filled with unfailing love. I knew how easily you could cancel your plans for destroying these people. Just kill me now, Lord! I'd rather be dead than alive because nothing I predicted is going to happen." The Lord replied, "Is it right for you to be angry about this?"

Examine your heart to see where you stand with God. Your heart cannot be godly if you are out of tune with God.

1 Peter 1:10 *This salvation was something the prophets wanted to know more about. They prophesied about this gracious salvation prepared for you, even though they had many questions as to what it all could mean.*

Respond in obedience regardless of your level of understanding. You need not know everything about plumbing to take a bath. You need not know everything about God to follow him.

Ecclesiastes 11:5 *God's ways are as hard to discern as the pathways of the wind, and as mysterious as a tiny baby being formed in a mother's womb.*

Wait for God to answer. Realize that the timing and level of the answer is up to his discretion. Rest in the knowledge that the Lord is God and he is acting in your best interests. The timing of answered prayer is as significant as the answer itself.

PROMISE FROM GOD:
1 Corinthians 14:33 *For God is not a God of disorder but of peace.*

Contentment

How can I find contentment regardless of life's circumstances?

2 Corinthians 12:10 *Since I know it is all for Christ's good, I am quite content with my weaknesses and with insults, hardships, persecutions, and calamities.*

2 Peter 1:3 *As we know Jesus better, his divine power gives us everything we need for living a godly life. He has called us to receive his own glory and goodness!*

When you depend on circumstances for your contentment, you become unhappy when things don't go your way. When you depend on Jesus for your contentment, you are secure because he never fails.

Matthew 5:3 *God blesses those who realize their need for him, for the Kingdom of Heaven is given to them.*

Luke 14:33 *So no one can become my disciple without giving up everything for me.*

Contentment comes when you are willing to give up everything for God. Only then are you truly free to rest in the peace and security God offers. Contentment is not how much you have, but what you do for God with what you have.

79

1 Timothy 6:6-7 *Yet true religion with contentment is great wealth. After all, we didn't bring anything with us when we came into the world, and we certainly cannot carry anything with us when we die.* Contentment comes from a proper perspective of eternity. Contentment is not how much you accumulate on earth as much as how much you send ahead to heaven.

What is the relationship between wealth and contentment?

Ecclesiastes 5:19-20 *To enjoy your work and accept your lot in life—that is indeed a gift from God. People who do this rarely look with sorrow on the past, for God has given them reasons for joy.*

Philippians 4:11-13 *I have learned how to get along happily whether I have much or little. . . . I have learned the secret of living in every situation. . . . For I can do everything with the help of Christ who gives me the strength I need.*

Hebrews 13:5 *Stay away from the love of money; be satisfied with what you have. For God has said, "I will never fail you. I will never forsake you."*
Contentment is not dependent on wealth, nor does it have to be stifled by poverty. Wealth by itself is neutral—neither good nor bad. The key is to thank God for what we have and to use our time and resources to please him.

1 Timothy 6:17 *Tell those who are rich in this world not to be proud and not to trust in their money, which will soon be gone. But their trust should be in the living God, who richly gives us all we need for our enjoyment.*

Ecclesiastes 5:10 *Those who love money will never have enough. How absurd to think that wealth brings true happiness!*
Money and possessions can easily deceive us into thinking, "If only I had a little more, I would be content." Nothing could be farther from the truth. Always wanting a bit more is a sign of discontent.

How do I find true peace and contentment in life?

Isaiah 26:3 *You will keep in perfect peace all who trust in you, whose thoughts are fixed on you!*
There are many ways to have peace or what you think is peace, but genuine peace is found only in a trusting relationship with the Lord. Peace is not the absence of conflict but the presence of God.

Is there a risk in being content?

Hosea 13:6 *But when you had eaten and were satisfied, then you became proud and forgot me.*
When contentment leads to complacency, we are in trouble. Enjoying God's blessings should lead

us to seek him and not forget him, to thank him and not ignore him.

PROMISE FROM GOD: Psalm 107:9 *For he satisfies the thirsty and fills the hungry with good things.*

Coping

How do I cope when life's pain becomes overwhelming?

Psalm 145:14 *The Lord helps the fallen and lifts up those bent beneath their loads.*

2 Corinthians 1:3 *All praise to the God and Father of our Lord Jesus Christ. He is the source of every mercy and the God who comforts us.*
When you are overwhelmed, God is there with mercy and comfort. Alone, you are downcast; with God, you are uplifted.

Isaiah 43:2 *When you go through deep waters and great trouble, I will be with you. When you go through rivers of difficulty, you will not drown! When you walk through the fire of oppression, you will not be burned up; the flames will not consume you.*
When you are overwhelmed, God is there with power to help you. Alone, you will drown in deep waters of difficulty; with God, you will prevail over floods or fires.

Psalm 61:2 *From the ends of the earth, I will cry to you for help, for my heart is overwhelmed. Lead me to the towering rock of safety.*
When you are overwhelmed, go to God in prayer. When the whole world seems to ignore you, God listens.

Psalm 55:22 *Give your burdens to the Lord, and he will take care of you. He will not permit the godly to slip and fall.*
When you are overwhelmed, trust him to care for you.

Psalm 71:14 *But I will keep on hoping for you to help me; I will praise you more and more.*

Psalm 42:5-6 *Why am I discouraged? Why so sad? I will put my hope in God! I will praise him again—my Savior and my God!*
When you are overwhelmed, hope in him and praise him.

Psalm 30:11-12 *You have turned my mourning into joyful dancing. You have taken away my clothes of mourning and clothed me with joy, that I might sing praises to you and not be silent. O Lord my God, I will give you thanks forever!*

Lamentations 3:32-33 *Though he brings grief, he also shows compassion according to the greatness of his unfailing love. For he does not enjoy hurting people or causing them sorrow.*

When you are overwhelmed, have confidence that you will recover with the Lord's help. With God, even the bitter seeds of tears, grief, and mourning may yield a harvest of joy and blessing.

How do I cope when life's demands seem impossible?

Matthew 19:26 *Jesus looked at them intently and said, "Humanly speaking, it is impossible. But with God everything is possible."*

Philippians 4:13 *For I can do everything with the help of Christ who gives me the strength I need.* Remember: what seems impossible for you is never impossible for God.

Psalm 33:17 *Don't count on your warhorse to give you victory—for all its strength, it cannot save you.*

Psalm 44:6 *I do not trust my bow; I do not count on my sword to save me.*

Psalm 39:7 *And so, Lord, where do I put my hope? My only hope is in you.*

Psalm 60:12 *With God's help we will do mighty things, for he will trample down our foes.* Remember: your ultimate hope should not be in anyone or anything other than the Lord. He alone can bring you through the pain safely to the other side.

Exodus 18:18, 21-24 *"You're going to wear yourself out—and the people, too. This job is too heavy a burden for you to handle all by yourself. . . . But find some capable, honest men who fear God and hate bribes. Appoint them as judges. . . . They will help you carry the load, making the task easier for you. If you follow this advice, and if God directs you to do so, then you will be able to endure the pressures, and all these people will go home in peace."* Moses listened to his father-in-law's advice and followed his suggestions.

Remember: it is important to follow God's directions. Many times seeking godly advice may provide a workable solution you had not considered. God's wisdom may flow to you through godly counselors.

1 Corinthians 15:58 *So, my dear brothers and sisters, be strong and steady, always enthusiastic about the Lord's work, for you know that nothing you do for the Lord is ever useless.*

1 Chronicles 28:20 *Then David continued, "Be strong and courageous, and do the work. Don't be afraid or discouraged by the size of the task, for the Lord God, my God, is with you. He will not fail you or forsake you. He will see to it that all the work related to the Temple of the Lord is finished correctly."* Remember: you can be strong, courageous, steady, enthusiastic, and confident of the Lord's presence. The demands of God's work are often

great, but when God is with you, you have reason to be strong and courageous.

How can I cope when others fail or hurt me?

Isaiah 2:22 *Stop putting your trust in mere humans. They are as frail as breath. How can they be of help to anyone?*
Realize that we each have the capacity to hurt one another.

Psalm 9:10 *Those who know your name trust in you, for you, O Lord, have never abandoned anyone who searches for you.*

2 Corinthians 4:9 *We are hunted down, but God never abandons us. We get knocked down, but we get up again and keep going.*
God is the only one who is perfect and whose promises are always true. He will never abandon you, hurt you, or fail to keep his promises. If you want a friend who will *never* fail you, try the One who will *always* be with you.

Psalm 142:1-3 *I cry out to the Lord; I plead for the Lord's mercy. I pour out my complaints before him and tell him all my troubles. For I am overwhelmed, and you alone know the way I should turn.*

Psalm 17:9 *Protect me from wicked people who attack me, from murderous enemies who surround me.*

Psalm 10:14 *But you do see the trouble and grief they cause. You take note of it and punish them. The helpless put their trust in you. You are the defender of orphans.*

Go to God for help. No one can compare with him.

Luke 23:34 *Jesus said, "Father, forgive these people, because they don't know what they are doing." And the soldiers gambled for his clothes by throwing dice.*

Matthew 6:14-15 *If you forgive those who sin against you, your heavenly Father will forgive you. But if you refuse to forgive others, your Father will not forgive your sins.*

Matthew 18:21-22 *Then Peter came to him and asked, "Lord, how often should I forgive someone who sins against me? Seven times?" "No!" Jesus replied, "seventy times seven!"*

Jesus is the perfect example of forgiveness, so his words are the perfect teaching about forgiveness.

1 Peter 3:9 *Don't repay evil for evil. Don't retaliate when people say unkind things about you. Instead, pay them back with a blessing. That is what God wants you to do, and he will bless you for it.*

Wait for the Lord to do things his way. God wants you to respond with a blessing rather than any act of retaliation. Evil is best overcome with good and justice, not with more evil.

2 Timothy 2:24 *The Lord's servants must not quarrel but must be kind to everyone. They must be*

able to teach effectively and be patient with difficult people.

Psalm 25:21 *May integrity and honesty protect me, for I put my hope in you.*

Be kind, patient, and honest. Have integrity and a true, right heart. Mutual kindness with integrity leads to mutual respect.

Colossians 3:13 *You must make allowance for each other's faults and forgive the person who offends you. Remember, the Lord forgave you, so you must forgive others.*

Be less sensitive to other's faults and wrongs toward you. You can do more about your own faults and wrongs toward others.

How can I cope with all my insecurities?

Psalm 139:17-18 *How precious are your thoughts about me, O God! They are innumerable! I can't even count them; they outnumber the grains of sand! And when I wake up in the morning, you are still with me!*

Matthew 10:29-31 *Not even a sparrow, worth only half a penny, can fall to the ground without your Father knowing it. And the very hairs on your head are all numbered. So don't be afraid; you are more valuable to him than a whole flock of sparrows.*

Realize how valuable you are to God.

Deuteronomy 31:8 *Do not be afraid or discouraged, for the Lord is the one who goes before you. He will be with you; he will neither fail you nor forsake you.*

Be aware of and take courage in his presence in your life. When God is with you, why should you fear anything?

Jeremiah 1:6-9 *"O Sovereign Lord," I said, "I can't speak for you! I'm too young!" "Don't say that," the Lord replied, "for you must go wherever I send you and say whatever I tell you. And don't be afraid of the people, for I will be with you and take care of you. I, the Lord, have spoken!" Then the Lord touched my mouth and said, "See, I have put my words in your mouth!"*

Obediently accept his assignments for you, realizing that he will provide strength wherever you are weak.

How can I help others cope?

2 Corinthians 1:4 *He comforts us in all our troubles so that we can comfort others. When others are troubled, we will be able to give them the same comfort God has given us.*

Be sensitive to those God brings into your life. He often provides opportunities for you to comfort others in circumstances similar to your own.

Job 42:11 *Then all his brothers, sisters, and former friends came and feasted with him in his home. And they consoled him and comforted him because of all the trials the Lord had brought against him. And each of them brought him a gift of money and a gold ring.*

Be present for those in need. There is a power of presence that exceeds even the power of words.

Job 21:2 *Listen closely to what I am saying. You can console me by listening to me.*

Listen to those who are struggling. A listening ear reflects a caring heart.

1 Corinthians 9:22 *When I am with those who are oppressed, I share their oppression so that I might bring them to Christ. Yes, I try to find common ground with everyone so that I might bring them to Christ.*

Empathize with others. A sympathetic heart recognizes another's problems; an empathetic heart shares those problems and helps bring others to Christ.

Proverbs 12:25 *Worry weighs a person down; an encouraging word cheers a person up.*

Proverbs 15:23 *Everyone enjoys a fitting reply; it is wonderful to say the right thing at the right time!*

Ephesians 4:29 *Let everything you say be good and helpful, so that your words will be an encouragement to those who hear them.*

Speak words that are encouraging, fitting, timely, good, and helpful.

PROMISE FROM GOD: Philippians 4:6-7 *Don't worry about anything; instead, pray about everything. Tell God what you need, and thank him for all he has done. If you do this, you will experience God's peace, which is far more wonderful than the human mind can understand. His peace will guard your hearts and minds as you live in Christ Jesus.*

Courage

Where do I get the courage to go on when life seems too hard or obstacles seem too big?

Psalm 27:1 *The Lord is my light and my salvation—so why should I be afraid?*

Isaiah 41:10 *Don't be afraid, for I am with you. Do not be dismayed, for I am your God. I will strengthen you. I will help you. I will uphold you with my victorious right hand.*

True courage comes from God, understanding that he is stronger than your mightiest foes and that he wants to use his strength to help you. Courage is not misplaced confidence in your weakness but well-placed confidence in God's strength.

How do I find the courage to face death?

Luke 12:4 *Dear friends, don't be afraid of those*

who want to kill you. They can only kill the body;
they cannot do any more to you.
When God is with you, you don't have to be
afraid of anything, even death.

1 Corinthians 15:54 *Death is swallowed up*
in victory.
By his resurrection, Jesus has won the victory
over death. Victory over death comes not from
a futile attempt to conquer death, but from
surrender to Jesus, who promises resurrection
and eternal life.

How do I find the courage to face change?

Genesis 46:3 *Do not be afraid to go down to*
Egypt, for I will see to it that you become a great
nation there.
Change may be part of God's plan for you. If so,
what you are headed into will give you joy and
satisfaction beyond your expectations. Remember, the greatest advances in life come through
change.

Exodus 4:13 *But Moses again pleaded, "Lord,*
please! Send someone else."
To experience fear is normal. To be paralyzed
by fear, however, can be an indication that you
doubt God's ability to care for you in the face
of change.

How do I find the courage to admit my mistakes?

2 Samuel 12:13 *Then David confessed to Nathan, "I have sinned against the Lord." Nathan replied, "Yes, but the Lord has forgiven you."*
To admit your mistakes and sins is to open the door to forgiveness and restoration of relationships. Hiding your mistakes and sins is planting them to grow a bigger harvest tomorrow.

How do I find the courage to stand firm in my convictions?

Esther 3:2 *But Mordecai refused to bow down or show [Haman] respect.*
Courage to stand firm in your convictions comes from understanding where your true loyalties lie. If you are more concerned about what others think than about what God thinks, you will find yourself lacking courage and wavering in your faith.

PROMISES FROM GOD: Joshua 1:9 *I command you—be strong and courageous! Do not be afraid or discouraged. For the Lord your God is with you wherever you go.*

Job 11:18 *You will have courage because you will have hope.*

Death

Is death really the end?

J o h n 1 1 : 2 5 - 2 6 *Jesus told her, "I am the resurrection and the life. Those who believe in me, even though they die like everyone else, will live again. They are given eternal life for believing in me and will never perish."*

1 C o r i n t h i a n s 1 5 : 5 4 - 5 5 *When this happens—when our perishable earthly bodies have been transformed into heavenly bodies that will never die—then at last the Scriptures will come true: "Death is swallowed up in victory. O death, where is your victory? O death, where is your sting?"*
For those who trust in Christ, death is not the end, but only the beginning of an eternity of infinite joy with the Lord.

How can I be certain that there is eternal life?

1 C o r i n t h i a n s 1 5 : 2 0 *But the fact is that Christ has been raised from the dead. He has become the first of a great harvest of those who will be raised to life again.*
Resurrection life is not just a theory. Jesus' resurrection guarantees the resurrection of everyone who trusts in him.

1 C o r i n t h i a n s 1 5 : 4 - 6 *He was buried, and he was raised from the dead on the third day, as*

the Scriptures said. He was seen by Peter and then by the twelve apostles. After that, he was seen by more than five hundred of his followers at one time, most of whom are still alive, though some have died by now.

The resurrection of Jesus is not mere religious myth. The biblical record mentions eyewitnesses to the risen Jesus and encourages people to interview them. Historical investigation serves only to confirm the fact of the resurrection. This, in turn, assures you of your eternal life.

What about people who haven't put their faith in Jesus? Is there any hope for them when they die?

John 3:16 *For God so loved the world that he gave his only Son, so that everyone who believes in him will not perish, but have eternal life.*

The only guarantee of eternal life after death is believing in Jesus. It is wise to examine our own hearts and make sure that we truly believe.

Luke 23:42-43 *Then he said, "Jesus, remember me when you come into your kingdom." And Jesus replied, "I assure you, today you will be with me in paradise."*

As with the thief on the cross and his simple faith, even at the last minute anyone can receive Jesus' assurance of eternal life. Therefore, since we do not know another person's every thought, there is always hope that a person turned to the Lord in the last minutes of life.

Is fear of death or thinking about death a bad thing?

Colossians 3:1-2 *Since you have been raised to new life with Christ, set your sights on the realities of heaven. . . . Let heaven fill your thoughts.*
Fear of the unknown is natural, and fear of death can be healthy if it draws us to know more about God and make every day count for him. The fear of death can lead us to victory over death if it leads us to surrender to Jesus, who has already conquered death.

Philippians 1:21 *For to me, living is for Christ, and dying is even better.*
Fear of dying may reveal a lack of trust in God's promises. Take time to ponder God's assurances of eternity and apply yourself to knowing and serving God. The more real God is to you, the less fearsome death will seem.

PROMISES FROM GOD: Psalm 49:15 *But as for me, God will redeem my life. He will snatch me from the power of death.*

Isaiah 25:8 *He will swallow up death forever!*

Matthew 10:28 *Don't be afraid of those who want to kill you. They can only kill your body; they cannot touch your soul.*

Depression

(*see also* DISCOURAGEMENT or SORROW)

What causes depression?

Job 30:16 *And now my heart is broken. Depression haunts my days.*

A broken heart is ripe for depression.

Ecclesiastes 4:8 *This is the case of a man who is all alone, without a child or a brother, yet who works hard to gain as much wealth as he can. But then he asks himself, "Who am I working for? Why am I giving up so much pleasure now?" It is all so meaningless and depressing.*

If we spend our lives pursuing meaningless things, we may become depressed as we recognize how meaningless those things truly are.

Proverbs 13:12 *Hope deferred makes the heart sick, but when dreams come true, there is life and joy.*

A heart without hope is ripe for depression. Hope lifts us up; depression drags us down.

1 Samuel 16:14 *Now the Spirit of the Lord had left Saul, and the Lord sent a tormenting spirit that filled him with depression and fear.*

If we depart from the Lord, depression can move easily into the vacant room in our hearts. The farther we move from God, the less hope we have of receiving his blessings.

Sometimes when I feel depressed it seems God doesn't care.

Psalm 139:12 *Even in darkness I cannot hide from you.*

There is no depth to which you can descend that God is not present with you. When depression comes, you must remember that even though you cannot see or feel his presence, he has not abandoned you.

Psalm 130:1 *From the depths of despair, O Lord, I call for your help.*

You can cry out to God in prayer even from the darkest night of despair. He will hear you.

Isaiah 53:3 *He was despised and rejected— a man of sorrows, acquainted with bitterest grief.*

Remember that through Christ God understands the pain of human life.

How should I handle depression?

Psalm 143:7 *Come quickly, Lord, and answer me, for my depression deepens. Don't turn away from me, or I will die.*

The Lord's strong presence in your life is the best cure for depression. You may also seek the best medical help and ask God to use it to heal you.

How does God bring healing to those who are depressed?

Psalm 10:17 *Lord, you know the hopes of the*

helpless. *Surely you will listen to their cries and comfort them.*

P s a l m   2 3 : 4 *Even when I walk through the dark valley of death, I will not be afraid, for you are close beside me. Your rod and your staff protect and comfort me.*

P s a l m   3 4 : 1 8 *The Lord is close to the broken-hearted; he rescues those who are crushed in spirit.* The power of the Lord's presence, coupled with the sensitivity of his listening ear, can bring healing and comfort.

Can any good come out of depression?

P s a l m   1 2 6 : 5 *Those who plant in tears will harvest with shouts of joy.*

N e h e m i a h   8 : 1 0 *Don't be dejected and sad, for the joy of the Lord is your strength!*

2   C o r i n t h i a n s   1 2 : 9 *My power works best in your weakness.*
When we are weak, we may be more receptive to the Lord's strength. When God works through our weakness, we know it is his work and not ours.

How can I help someone who is depressed?

2   C o r i n t h i a n s   1 : 4 *He comforts us in all our troubles so that we can comfort others. When others are troubled, we will be able to give them the same comfort God has given us.*

Romans 12:15 *When others are happy, be happy with them. If they are sad, share their sorrow.*

Proverbs 25:20 *Singing cheerful songs to a person whose heart is heavy is as bad as stealing someone's jacket in cold weather or rubbing salt in a wound.*

Two things help most: modeling the gentle, caring love of Christ, and directing the depressed person to the proper care. Those dealing with depression need comfort and understanding, not advice and lectures. You can help someone who is depressed by your quiet presence, your love, and your encouragement. Telling them to "snap out of it" only makes things worse.

Are feelings of depression sin?

Isaiah 24:16 *Listen to them as they sing to the Lord from the ends of the earth. Hear them singing praises to the Righteous One! But my heart is heavy with grief. I am discouraged, for evil still prevails, and treachery is everywhere.*

The flames of moral outrage at the presence of terrible sin can leave the ashes of depression. This is not a sin.

John 12:27 *Now my soul is deeply troubled. Should I pray, "Father, save me from what lies ahead?" But that is the very reason why I came!*

In the very process of redemption Jesus felt deeply troubled, or quite "low." It is natural

to feel low in the backwash of troubled times.
Since Jesus cannot sin, to feel low or depressed
cannot be a sin. It can be a result of sin or
become a sin if we blame God, use it against
God, or leave God out of our antidote.

Does feeling depressed mean something is wrong with my faith?

Judges 15:18 *Now Samson was very thirsty,
and he cried out to the Lord, "You have accomplished
this great victory. . . . Must I now die of thirst?"*

1 Kings 19:3-4 *Elijah was afraid and fled for
his life. . . . He sat down under a solitary broom tree
and prayed that he might die.*

Matthew 14:30-31 *When he looked around at
the high waves, he was terrified and began to sink.
"Save me, Lord!" he shouted. Instantly Jesus reached
out his hand and grabbed him.*
Even for the people of God, depression can often
follow great achievement or spiritual victory.

PROMISE FROM GOD: Matthew
11:28 *Then Jesus said, "Come to me, all of you
who are weary and carry heavy burdens, and I will
give you rest."*

Disappointment

How should I handle my disappointment with God?

Exodus 5:22 *So Moses went back to the Lord and protested.*
Go to God in prayer to try to understand his ways.

John 11:21 *Martha said to Jesus, "Lord, if you had been here, my brother would not have died."*
Be honest with God about your thoughts and feelings. He knows them anyway, so why try to hide them?

2 Corinthians 12:8-10 *Three different times I begged the Lord to take it away. Each time he said, "My gracious favor is all you need. My power works best in your weakness." So now I am glad to boast about my weaknesses, so that the power of Christ may work through me. . . . For when I am weak, then I am strong.*
We cannot understand why God doesn't always take away our pain, but we do know that our weaknesses are great opportunities for God to work his power through us. Even Jesus purchased our redemption through suffering. Why should we expect to purchase redemptive living more cheaply?

How should I deal with life's disappointments?

Psalm 63:1 *O God, you are my God; I earnestly search for you. My soul thirsts for you.*
In your disappointment, move toward God, not away from him. Running from the one who can help you is not wise.

Is there a way to avoid or minimize disappointment?

Haggai 1:6, 9 *You have planted much but harvested little. . . . Why? Because my house lies in ruins, says the Lord Almighty, while you are all busy building your own fine houses.*
Put God first. Give him the first part of your money, the best minutes of your day, the highest priority in your life. By doing this you will learn to see what is truly important, and you will discover that there is nothing more rewarding and satisfying than a relationship with the God who created you and loves you.

Psalm 22:5 *You heard their cries for help and saved them. They put their trust in you and were never disappointed.*

Psalm 34:2 *I will boast only in the Lord; let all who are discouraged take heart.*
Put your faith, trust, and expectations in the Lord. Because he created you, you can only learn from him what he has planned for you.

Galatians 6:9 *So don't get tired of doing what is good. Don't get discouraged and give up, for we will reap a harvest of blessing at the appropriate time.* Maintain the joy of doing God's good work.

Galatians 6:4 *Be sure to do what you should, for then you will enjoy the personal satisfaction of having done your work well, and you won't need to compare yourself to anyone else.* Do what is right, and the satisfaction of a job well done will minimize disappointment.

PROMISE FROM GOD: Psalm 55:22 *Give your burdens to the Lord, and he will take care of you.*

Discouragement

(*see also* DEPRESSION or ENCOURAGEMENT or SORROW)

How can I handle discouragement?

1 Peter 5:8-9 *Watch out for attacks from the Devil. . . . Take a firm stand against him, and be strong in your faith. Remember that Christians all over the world are going through the same kind of suffering you are.* When you are discouraged, you are particularly vulnerable to Satan's attacks. Be especially careful

104

to stay close to God's Word and other believers during these difficult times.

1 Samuel 1:10 *Hannah was in deep anguish, crying bitterly as she prayed to the Lord.*
Prayer is the first step you must take when discouraged, for it moves you into the presence of God.

2 Chronicles 20:15 *Don't be discouraged by this mighty army, for the battle is not yours, but God's.*
It would have been easy for the people of Judah to see only the vast enemy army and not see God standing by to destroy it. Be careful to disconnect your feelings of discouragement from your assurance of God's love for you. Discouragement can cause you to doubt God's love, drawing you away from the source of your greatest help.

PROMISE FROM GOD: Galatians 6:9 *Don't get discouraged and give up, for we will reap a harvest of blessing at the appropriate time.*

Doubt

(*see also* CONFIDENCE or FAITH)

Is it a sin to doubt God?
Psalm 94:19 *When doubts filled my mind, your comfort gave me renewed hope and cheer.*

Matthew 14:31 *Instantly Jesus reached out his hand and grabbed him. "You don't have much faith," Jesus said. "Why did you doubt me?"*
David and Peter—along with many other biblical heroes—struggled with doubt. God doesn't mind doubt as long as we are seeking him in the midst of it. Doubt is sin if it leads us from God or if we allow it to turn to skepticism, then to cynicism, then to hardheartedness. But doubt is a blessing if it leads us to God and if we allow it to become honest searching, and then faith.

What should I do when I find myself doubting?

Habakkuk 1:2 *How long, O Lord, must I call for help?*
Bring your doubts directly to God in prayer. Be candid and passionate as you pour out your heart to the Lord. Thus, even doubt can draw you closer to him.

Mark 9:24 *The father instantly replied, "I do believe, but help me not to doubt!"*
Pray that God will give you the fullness of faith that you need.

Mark 8:17-19 *Why are you so worried about having no food? . . . Don't you remember anything at all? What about the five thousand men I fed with five loaves of bread?*
When you are struggling with experiential doubt,

take time to remember the way God has worked—
in the Bible and in your life. As you bring to mind
God's track record, you will grow confident that he
is real and will work in your present situation.

*John 20:27 Then he said to Thomas, "Put your
finger here and see my hands. Put your hand into the
wound in my side."*
When you have intellectual doubts, check out
the evidence.

*Habakkuk 2:1 I will climb up into my watch-
tower now and wait to see what the Lord will say to
me and how he will answer my complaint.*
Be patient. Let God answer your questions on his
schedule, not yours. Don't throw away your faith
just because God doesn't resolve your doubt
immediately.

PROMISE FROM GOD: Hebrews
13:5 *For God has said, "I will never fail you. I will
never forsake you."*

Emotions

Is it OK to be open with my emotions?
*Ezra 3:12 Many of the older priests, Levites, and
other leaders remembered the first Temple, and they
wept aloud when they saw the new Temple's foundation. The others, however, were shouting for joy.*

2 Samuel 18:33 *The king was overcome with emotion. He went up to his room over the gateway and burst into tears. And as he went, he cried, "O my son Absalom! My son, my son Absalom! If only I could have died instead of you! O Absalom, my son, my son."*
It is not a sign of weakness to display your emotions. It is, rather, a sign of your humanity and an important component of your emotional health.

Job 7:11 *I cannot keep from speaking. I must express my anguish. I must complain in my bitterness.*
Keep an open dialogue with the Lord and others you trust so you are not covering up your emotions.

Matthew 26:38 *He told them, "My soul is crushed with grief to the point of death. Stay here and watch with me."*
Jesus was honest with his disciples about his deep emotions. You also need this openness with trusted friends.

How can I keep my emotions from controlling my actions?

Psalm 119:101, 105 *I have refused to walk on any path of evil, that I may remain obedient to your word. . . . Your word is a lamp for my feet and a light for my path.*
Make a firm resolution that God's Word, not

108

what you feel like doing, will be the standard for your actions. Before you act, ask yourself whether what you are about to do is in line with the Bible's teaching.

Ephesians 4:26-27 *And "don't sin by letting anger gain control over you." Don't let the sun go down while you are still angry, for anger gives a mighty foothold to the Devil.*
Don't let anger fester. Deal promptly with the situations that cause you to be angry or else anger will conquer you.

Proverbs 4:23 *Above all else, guard your heart, for it affects everything you do.*
Your heart is the wellspring of your emotions. Don't put little bandages on your emotions when you can let Jesus transform your heart.

Ephesians 4:31-32 *Get rid of all bitterness, rage, anger, harsh words, and slander, as well as all types of malicious behavior. Instead, be kind to each other, tenderhearted, forgiving one another, just as God through Christ has forgiven you.*
Bitterness and resentment can control you unless you truly forgive the person who has wronged you.

PROMISE FROM GOD: Galatians 5:22-23 *But when the Holy Spirit controls our lives, he will produce this kind of fruit in us: love, joy, peace, patience, kindness, goodness, faithfulness, gentleness, and self-control.*

Encouragement

How does God encourage me?

1 Kings 19:4-6 *Then he went on alone into the desert, traveling all day. He sat down under a solitary broom tree and prayed that he might die. "I have had enough, Lord," he said. . . . But as he was sleeping, an angel touched him and told him, "Get up and eat!" He looked around and saw some bread baked on hot stones and a jar of water!*
He meets your needs at just the right time.

Psalm 138:3 *When I pray, you answer me; you encourage me by giving me the strength I need.*
He gives you strength when you ask.

Psalm 119:25, 28 *I lie in the dust, completely discouraged; revive me by your word. . . . I weep with grief; encourage me by your word.*

Romans 15:4 *Such things were written in the Scriptures long ago to teach us. They give us hope and encouragement as we wait patiently for God's promises.*
He's given his written Word to revive you and offer you hope.

Matthew 9:2 *Some people brought to him a paralyzed man on a mat. Seeing their faith, Jesus said to the paralyzed man, "Take heart, son! Your sins are forgiven."*
He forgives your sins.

Hebrews 12:5 *And have you entirely forgotten the encouraging words God spoke to you, his children? He said, "My child, don't ignore it when the Lord disciplines you, and don't be discouraged when he corrects you."*
Even his discipline is an encouragement, for you know it is for your ultimate good.

How can I be an encouragement to others?

1 Samuel 23:16 *Jonathan went to find David and encouraged him to stay strong in his faith in God.*
By helping them keep a close relationship with God.

Ephesians 4:29 *Don't use foul or abusive language. Let everything you say be good and helpful, so that your words will be an encouragement to those who hear them.*
By making sure everything you say is kind and uplifting.

2 Chronicles 32:8 *"He may have a great army, but they are just men. We have the Lord our God to help us and to fight our battles for us!" These words greatly encouraged the people.*
By reminding them of what God can do, and wants to do, for and through them.

2 Chronicles 30:22 *Hezekiah encouraged the Levites for the skill they displayed as they served the Lord.*
By complimenting them for a job well done.

Titus 1:9 *He must have a strong and steadfast belief in the trustworthy message he was taught; then he will be able to encourage others with right teaching and show those who oppose it where they are wrong.*
By sharing God's instruction and correction with them.

Job 29:24 *When they were discouraged, I smiled at them. My look of approval was precious to them.*
By smiling at them!

Ezra 5:1-2 *Haggai and Zechariah son of Iddo prophesied in the name of the God of Israel to the Jews in Judah and Jerusalem. Zerubbabel . . . responded by beginning the task of rebuilding the Temple.*
By encouraging them to once again get involved in productive work.

Acts 11:23 *[Barnabas] encouraged the believers to stay true to the Lord.*
By encouraging them to hold fast to the principles of faith and to take action with those principles. Encouragement is more than hollow praise. Barnabas is known as the "great encourager" in the Bible. His encouragement of John Mark helped Mark become a faithful disciple.

Philemon 11 *Now he is very useful to both of us.*
By showing your trust in them.

Philippians 1:6 *And I am sure that God, who began the good work within you, will continue his work until it is finally finished.*
By affirming them and the work they are doing for God. Affirmation is a seal of approval on words of encouragement.

Joshua 24:13 *I gave you land you had not worked for, and I gave you cities you did not build.*
By encouraging them to review God's past blessings.

PROMISE FROM GOD:
2 Thessalonians 2:16-17 *May our Lord Jesus Christ and God our Father . . . comfort your hearts and give you strength in every good thing you do and say.*

Endurance

(see also PERSEVERANCE)

Why should I keep on trying when I feel like quitting?

1 Timothy 6:11 *But you, Timothy, belong to God; so run from all these evil things, and follow what is right and good. Pursue a godly life, along with faith, love, perseverance, and gentleness.*

1 Peter 2:20 *Of course, you get no credit for being patient if you are beaten for doing wrong. But*

if you suffer for doing right and are patient beneath the blows, God is pleased with you.

Revelation 13:10 *The people who are destined for prison will be arrested and taken away. Those who are destined for death will be killed. But do not be dismayed, for here is your opportunity to have endurance and faith.*

Endurance is commanded and commended by God. It is necessary to reach the goal of a life well lived and, ultimately, of eternal life.

Mark 13:13 *And everyone will hate you because of your allegiance to me. But those who endure to the end will be saved.*

2 Timothy 2:12 *If we endure hardship, we will reign with him. If we deny him, he will deny us.*

Endurance is the sign that your faith is for real because it shows that you have eternal goals clearly in mind. The more you stop, the longer and harder it is to get where you are going.

How do I develop endurance?

2 Corinthians 1:8-9 *I think you ought to know, dear brothers and sisters, about the trouble we went through in the province of Asia. We were crushed and completely overwhelmed, and we thought we would never live through it. In fact, we expected to die. But as a result, we learned not to rely on ourselves, but on God who can raise the dead.*

2 Thessalonians 3:5 *May the Lord bring you into an ever deeper understanding of the love of God and the endurance that comes from Christ.*

Ephesians 6:13 *Use every piece of God's armor to resist the enemy in the time of evil, so that after the battle you will still be standing firm.*
Endurance originates with God. He is your source of the power and perseverance you need to endure.

Hebrews 12:2-3 *We do this by keeping our eyes on Jesus, on whom our faith depends from start to finish. He was willing to die a shameful death on the cross because of the joy he knew would be his afterward. Now he is seated in the place of highest honor beside God's throne in heaven. Think about all he endured when sinful people did such terrible things to him, so that you don't become weary and give up.*
You have the example of Jesus on which to focus as your model for endurance. The next time you are tempted to give up, think of Jesus on the cross.

Romans 5:3 *We can rejoice, too, when we run into problems and trials, for we know that they are good for us—they help us learn to endure.*

James 1:2-4 *Dear brothers and sisters, whenever trouble comes your way, let it be an opportunity for joy. For when your faith is tested, your endurance has a chance to grow. So let it grow, for when your endurance is fully developed, you will be strong in character and ready for anything.*

Of course you don't like problems, trials, troubles, and the testing of your faith, for they can drag you down. But they can also lift you up, and when they do, you have learned endurance.

What are the benefits of endurance?

1 Peter 2:19 *For God is pleased with you when, for the sake of your conscience, you patiently endure unfair treatment.*

Endurance pleases God.

James 5:11 *We give great honor to those who endure under suffering. Job is an example of a man who endured patiently. From his experience we see how the Lord's plan finally ended in good, for he is full of tenderness and mercy.*

Endurance honors God and his plan for you.

1 Peter 4:13 *Instead, be very glad—because these trials will make you partners with Christ in his suffering, and afterward you will have the wonderful joy of sharing his glory when it is displayed to all the world.*

Matthew 24:13 *But those who endure to the end will be saved.*

Hebrews 10:36 *Patient endurance is what you need now, so you will continue to do God's will. Then you will receive all that he has promised.*

James 1:12 *God blesses the people who patiently endure testing. Afterward they will receive the crown of life that God has promised to those who love him.*

2 Timothy 4:7-8 *I have fought a good fight, I have finished the race, and I have remained faithful. And now the prize awaits me—the crown of righteousness that the Lord, the righteous Judge, will give me on that great day of his return.*

Endurance makes you a partner with Christ in his suffering and in his glory.

James 1:2-4 *Dear brothers and sisters, whenever trouble comes your way, let it be an opportunity for joy. For when your faith is tested, your endurance has a chance to grow. So let it grow, for when your endurance is fully developed, you will be strong in character and ready for anything.*

1 Peter 1:7 *These trials are only to test your faith, to show that it is strong and pure. It is being tested as fire tests and purifies gold—and your faith is far more precious to God than mere gold. So if your faith remains strong after being tried by fiery trials, it will bring you much praise and glory and honor on the day when Jesus Christ is revealed to the whole world.*

Endurance produces godliness, love, productivity, usefulness, growth, strength of character, preparedness, strong faith, and eternal rewards.

2 Corinthians 1:6 *So when we are weighed down with troubles, it is for your benefit and salvation! For when God comforts us, it is so that we, in turn, can be an encouragement to you. Then you can patiently endure the same things we suffer.*

Revelation 1:9 *I am John, your brother. In Jesus we are partners in suffering and in the Kingdom and in patient endurance. I was exiled to the island of Patmos for preaching the word of God and speaking about Jesus.*
Endurance encourages others, for it leads others to follow your example.

PROMISE FROM GOD: Galatians 6:9 *So don't get tired of doing what is good. Don't get discouraged and give up, for we will reap a harvest of blessing at the appropriate time.*

Enthusiasm

How can I regain my enthusiasm for life and faith?

Colossians 3:23 *Work hard and cheerfully at whatever you do, as though you were working for God rather than for people.*
Your attitude improves when you do even life's most distasteful or onerous duties as a praise

offering to the Lord. How can you disdain what you joyfully offer to God?

Psalm 103:2 *Praise the Lord, I tell myself, and never forget the good things he does for me.*
Counting your blessings will increase your enthusiasm. Forgetting your blessings will lead to apathy.

Mark 6:31 *Then Jesus said, "Let's get away from the crowds for a while and rest."*
Taking care of your body through proper rest, nutrition, and exercise will have a positive impact on your outlook on life.

2 Corinthians 9:2 *In fact, it was your enthusiasm that stirred up many of them to begin helping.*
Choose to spend time with enthusiastic people. Their spirit will rub off on you because enthusiasm is contagious!

Psalm 9:2 *I will be filled with joy because of you. I will sing praises to your name, O Most High.*
Focus on the Lord and worship him, even if you don't feel like it, and your enthusiasm will increase.

PROMISE FROM GOD: Psalm 51:12 *Restore to me again the joy of your salvation, and make me willing to obey you.*

Evil

(*see also* SIN)

If God is good, why does he let people do evil things?

Genesis 2:15-17 *The Lord God placed the man in the Garden of Eden to tend and care for it. But the Lord God gave him this warning: "You may freely eat any fruit in the garden except fruit from the tree of the knowledge of good and evil. If you eat of its fruit, you will surely die."*

Genuine love requires the freedom to choose. From the beginning, God desired a loving relationship with humans, so he gave us this freedom. But with ability to make choices comes the possibility of choosing our own way over God's way. Our own way always leads to sin. This breaks God's heart, but the alternative is making us robots, not humans.

Where does evil come from?

Jeremiah 17:9 *The human heart is most deceitful and desperately wicked. Who really knows how bad it is?*

Our own hearts, polluted by sin and selfishness, are the source of much that is evil.

Ephesians 6:12 *For we are not fighting against people made of flesh and blood, but against the evil*

*rulers and authorities of the unseen world, against
those mighty powers of darkness who rule this world,
against wicked spirits in the heavenly realms.*
Cosmic forces of evil, led by Satan, are engaged
in a deadly rebellion against God.

How can I combat evil?

Romans 12:9 *Hate what is wrong. Stand on the
side of good.*
Start by resolving to hate everything that is sinful
and evil.

Romans 13:14 *But let the Lord Jesus Christ take
control of you, and don't think of ways to indulge your
evil desires.*
Surrender yourself to Christ's control. Make sure
that you don't put yourself in situations where
you know your resolve for righteousness will be
tested. The closer you walk with Christ, the
harder it is to be caught in the snare of evil.

Ephesians 6:10-11 *A final word: Be strong
with the Lord's mighty power. Put on all of God's
armor so that you will be able to stand firm against
all strategies and tricks of the Devil.*
Your own strength is insufficient to combat evil.
With God's strength and protection, however,
you can win the battle.

Romans 12:21 *Don't let evil get the best of you,
but conquer evil by doing good.*

It often seems that evil is winning; can this really be?

John 16:33 *Here on earth you will have many trials and sorrows. But take heart, because I have overcome the world.*

It will appear at times that evil has the upper hand. But the Lord's power is supreme, and he will win the victory.

Revelation 21:4 *He will remove all of their sorrows, and there will be no more death or sorrow or crying or pain. For the old world and its evils are gone forever.*

When Jesus returns to usher in eternity, he will eradicate evil forever. No matter how bleak things may seem now, we are on the winning side!

Why do people often seem to get away with evil?

Psalm 73:17-20 *Then one day I went into your sanctuary, O God, and I thought about the destiny of the wicked. Truly, you put them on a slippery path and send them sliding over the cliff to destruction. In an instant they are destroyed, swept away by terrors. Their present life is only a dream that is gone when they awake.*

All of us will someday stand before God's judgment seat. The present prosperity of evildoers is only temporary.

Isaiah 32:7-8 *The smooth tricks of evil people will be exposed, including all the lies they use to oppress the poor in the courts. But good people will be generous to others and will be blessed for all they do.* It seems that people today can do anything they want and not only get away with it, but flourish. God has promised, however, that in his time everyone will be judged, evil will be exposed, and the righteous will prevail. If righteousness always prevailed on earth, then people wouldn't be following God for the right reasons—they would follow God only to have an easy life. God doesn't promise the absence of evil on this earth. In fact, he guarantees that evil will be pervasive and powerful. But God promises to help us stand against evil, and if we do, we will receive our reward of eternal life with him in heaven, where evil will be no more.

PROMISE FROM GOD: Psalm 1:6 *For the Lord watches over the path of the godly, but the path of the wicked leads to destruction.*

Failure

Everyone else seems so successful; am I the only one who fails?

1 Samuel 8:1, 3 *As Samuel grew old, he appointed his sons to be judges over Israel. . . . But*

they were not like their father, for they were greedy for money.

2 Samuel 12:13 *Then David confessed to Nathan, "I have sinned against the Lord."*

Luke 22:59-62 *Someone else insisted, "This must be one of Jesus' disciples. . . ." But Peter said, "Man, I don't know what you are talking about." And as soon as he said these words, the rooster crowed. . . . Then Peter remembered that the Lord had said, "Before the rooster crows tomorrow morning, you will deny me three times." And Peter left the courtyard, crying bitterly.*

No one is exempt from failing. Even the heroes of the Bible like Samuel, David, and Peter had firsthand experiences with failure. Failing does not mean you are substandard—only human.

When I have failed, how do I get past it and go on?

1 Kings 8:33-34 *If your people Israel are defeated by their enemies because they have sinned against you, and if they turn to you and call on your name and pray to you here in this Temple, then hear from heaven and forgive their sins and return them to this land you gave their ancestors.*

Turning to God in repentance and trust is the best response you can have to your failure.

Micah 7:8 *Though I fall, I will rise again. Though I sit in darkness, the Lord himself will be my light.*

2 Corinthians 4:9 *We are hunted down, but God never abandons us. We get knocked down, but we get up again and keep going.*

The best response to failure is to get up again, holding on to the hope that God gives you through faith.

1 Corinthians 10:6-7 *These events happened as a warning to us, so that we would not crave evil things as they did or worship idols as some of them did.*

Remember that failure can be helpful; it can teach you important lessons about what to avoid in the future. You need not repeat your mistakes or the mistakes you recognize in others!

2 Timothy 2:12 *If we endure hardship, we will reign with him.*

Failure doesn't have to be the end—it can be a beginning. You can recover and move on. There is a way out.

PROMISE FROM GOD: Psalm 37:23-24 *The steps of the godly are directed by the Lord. He delights in every detail of their lives. Though they stumble, they will not fall, for the Lord holds them by the hand.*

Faith

Faith seems so complicated; how can I ever get it?

Mark 5:36 *But Jesus ignored their comments and said to Jairus, "Don't be afraid. Just trust me."*
Faith isn't complicated. It simply means trusting Jesus to do what he has promised.

Psalm 131:2 *But I have stilled and quieted myself, just as a small child is quiet with its mother. Yes, like a small child is my soul within me.*
It is not hard for a little child to attain faith. The child simply lives with the calm assurance of his parent's provision and protection. You can have this same uncomplicated trust in God.

How can I strengthen my faith?

Genesis 12:1, 4 *Then the Lord told Abram, "Leave your country. . . ." So Abram departed as the Lord had instructed him.*
Like a muscle, faith gets stronger the more you exercise it. When you follow God and see him come through for you, your faith is stronger when you encounter the next trial or test.

Psalm 119:48, 54 *I honor and love your commands. I meditate on your principles. . . . Your principles have been the music of my life throughout the years of my pilgrimage.*

Your faith will grow stronger as you study the Bible and reflect on the truths it sets forth about who God is and his guidelines for your life.

When I'm struggling in my Christian life and have doubts, does it mean I have less faith?

Genesis 15:8 *But Abram replied, "O Sovereign Lord, how can I be sure that you will give it to me?"*

Matthew 11:2-3 *John the Baptist . . . sent his disciples to ask Jesus, "Are you really the Messiah we've been waiting for?"*
Many people in the Bible whom we consider to be "pillars of faith" had moments of doubt. The key is to bring your doubts directly to the Lord. Doubts are good when they bring you closer to God.

PROMISES FROM GOD: Acts 16:31 *They replied, "Believe on the Lord Jesus and you will be saved, along with your entire household."*

2 Thessalonians 1:10 *And you will be among those praising him on that day, for you believed what we testified about him.*

1 Peter 1:7 *So if your faith remains strong after being tried by fiery trials, it will bring you much praise and glory and honor on the day when Jesus Christ is revealed to the whole world.*

1 John 5:4 *For every child of God defeats this evil world by trusting Christ to give the victory.*

Fear

What can I do when I am overcome with fear?

Psalm 46:1-2 *God is our refuge and strength, always ready to help in times of trouble. So we will not fear, even if earthquakes come and the mountains crumble into the sea.*

Deuteronomy 31:6 *Be strong and courageous! Do not be afraid of them! The Lord your God will go ahead of you. He will neither fail you nor forsake you.* Remind yourself that God is always with you. Your situation may be genuinely threatening, but God has not abandoned you and he promises to stay with you. Even if your situation is so bad that it causes death, God has not left you but has instead ushered you into his very presence.

Philippians 4:6-7 *Do not worry about anything, but in everything with prayer and supplication with thanksgiving let your requests be made known to God. And the peace of God, which surpasses all understanding, will guard your hearts and your minds in Christ Jesus.* Pray with a thankful heart, asking God to give you what you need to deal with your fears. Peace is not the absence of fear but the conquest of fear. Peace is not running away, but overcoming.

Is fear ever good?

Psalm 2:11 *Serve the Lord with reverent fear, and rejoice with trembling.*

Because God is so great and mighty and because he holds the power of life and death in his hands, we must have a healthy, reverent fear of him. A healthy fear of God recognizes what he could do if he gave us what we deserved. But we rejoice when we recognize that instead he gives us mercy and forgiveness. A healthy fear should drive us to God for his mercy and help us keep our perspective about where we need to be in our relationship with God.

Deuteronomy 31:7-8 *Be strong and courageous! . . . Do not be afraid or discouraged, for the Lord is the one who goes before you.*

Fear can be good if it teaches us about courage. Joshua couldn't have truly understood courage if he hadn't experienced fear. Fear gave him courageous character and taught him to rely on and trust in God.

PROMISES FROM GOD: Isaiah 41:10 *Don't be afraid, for I am with you. Do not be dismayed, for I am your God. I will strengthen you. I will help you. I will uphold you with my victorious right hand.*

Leviticus 26:6 *I will give you peace in the land, and you will be able to sleep without fear.*

Financial Difficulties

(*see also* POVERTY)

What are some of God's principles for financial health?

Proverbs 13:11 *Wealth from get-rich-quick schemes quickly disappears; wealth from hard work grows.*

Trying to get rich quickly usually backfires. Dedicate yourself to hard work over time. If something seems too good to be true, it probably is.

Proverbs 22:7 *Just as the rich rule the poor, so the borrower is servant to the lender.*

Undisciplined use of credit is a recipe for ruin.

Proverbs 23:20-21 *Do not carouse with drunkards and gluttons, for they are on their way to poverty. Too much sleep clothes a person with rags.*

If you have lots of money, don't let it affect the way God wants you to live.

Proverbs 6:10-11 *A little extra sleep, a little more slumber, a little folding of the hands to rest— and poverty will pounce on you like a bandit; scarcity will attack you like a robber.*

Initiative, energy, and self-discipline are essential for financial health. Laziness doesn't put money in the bank.

PROMISE FROM GOD: Philippians 4 : 1 9 *And this same God who takes care of me will supply all your needs from his glorious riches, which have been given to us in Christ Jesus.*

Forgiveness

(*see also* GUILT or REPENTANCE or SIN)

Can any sin be forgiven? There must be some sins that are too great to be forgiven.

M a r k   3 : 2 8   *I assure you that any sin can be forgiven.*

R o m a n s   8 : 3 8   *Nothing can ever separate us from his love.*

Forgiveness is not based on the magnitude of the sin, but the magnitude of the forgiver's love. No sin is too great for God's complete and unconditional love.

Is there an unforgivable sin?

M a t t h e w   1 2 : 3 1   *Every sin or blasphemy can be forgiven—except blasphemy against the Holy Spirit, which can never be forgiven.*

Blasphemy against the Holy Spirit is called an unforgivable sin. The reason it is unforgivable is because it reflects a settled, hardhearted attitude of defiant hostility toward God. A person who has that attitude will never come to God for forgiveness—so such a sin is unforgivable. If you're worried about whether you've committed the unforgivable sin, it's highly unlikely.

What does it really mean that I am forgiven?

Colossians 1:22 *You are holy and blameless as you stand before him without a single fault.*

Isaiah 1:18 *No matter how deep the stain of your sins, I can remove it. I can make you as clean as freshly fallen snow.*

Forgiveness means that God looks at you as though you have never sinned. You are blameless before him. When God forgives, he doesn't sweep your sins under the carpet; instead, he completely washes them away.

Romans 4:7 *Oh, what joy for those whose disobedience is forgiven, whose sins are put out of sight.*

Forgiveness brings great joy.

How do I experience forgiveness when I have done wrong?

Psalm 51:4 *Against you, and you alone, have I sinned; I have done what is evil in your sight.*

You must realize that God is the one who has been wronged by your sin, so he is the one you first ask for forgiveness.

Ezra 10:11 *Confess your sin to the Lord, the God of your ancestors, and do what he demands.*

1 John 1:8-9 *If we say we have no sin, we are only fooling ourselves and refusing to accept the truth.*

But if we confess our sins to him, he is faithful and just to forgive us and to cleanse us from every wrong. You will receive God's forgiveness when you confess your sins to him, stop doing what is wrong, and turn to him with your whole heart.

A c t s 1 3 : 3 8 *In this man Jesus there is forgiveness for your sins.*
You receive God's forgiveness by trusting in Christ as your Savior and Lord.

How can I forgive someone who has hurt me very badly?

E p h e s i a n s 4 : 3 1 *Get rid of all bitterness, rage, anger, harsh words, and slander, as well as all types of malicious behavior.*
Remember that unforgiveness not only ruins your relationships, but it also poisons your soul. The person most hurt by unforgiveness is you.

R o m a n s 1 2 : 1 9 *Dear friends, never avenge yourselves. Leave that to God. For it is written, "I will take vengeance; I will repay those who deserve it," says the Lord.*
Punishing evildoers is God's job, not yours, and God can be trusted to do his job. Therefore, you can remove yourself from the endless cycle of revenge and retaliation by forgiving.

PROMISE FROM GOD: J e r e m i a h 3 : 2 2 *"My wayward children," says the Lord, "come back to me, and I will heal your wayward hearts."*

Fulfillment

(*see also* MEANING or PURPOSE or
LONELINESS)

Will God really fill the emptiness of my life?

John 6:35 *Jesus replied, "I am the bread of life. No one who comes to me will ever be hungry again. Those who believe in me will never thirst."*

Jesus is the nourishment your soul craves. He truly satisfies your deepest hunger by meeting your needs, working in your life, carrying out his plans for you, and offering you peace of mind and eternal life.

John 4:13-14 *Jesus replied, "People soon become thirsty again after drinking this water. But the water I give them takes away thirst altogether. It becomes a perpetual spring within them, giving them eternal life."*

Jesus fills your emptiness with his presence. He fills your life, now and forever.

PROMISE FROM GOD: Psalm 103: 5 *He fills my life with good things.*

Future

How can I face the future when it is so uncertain?

Hebrews 13:8 *Jesus Christ is the same yesterday, today, and forever.*

Psalm 121:8 *The Lord keeps watch over you as you come and go, both now and forever.*
You can face the uncertain future because you have an unchanging God who loves and guides you. As the old saying puts it: We know not what the future holds, but we know who holds the future.

Matthew 6:34 *So don't worry about tomorrow, for tomorrow will bring its own worries. Today's trouble is enough for today.*
Most of the things we worry might happen never do. So don't waste time on the "what-if" worries. Spend your worry time as prayer time.

What are some promises I can look forward to in my future with God?

1 John 3:2 *Yes, dear friends, we are already God's children, and we can't even imagine what we will be like when Christ returns. But we do know that when he comes we will be like him, for we will see him as he really is.*
You will one day be like Christ.

Jeremiah 29:11 *"For I know the plans I have for you," says the Lord. "They are plans for good and not for disaster, to give you a future and a hope."* The great plans God has for you will some day be revealed and fulfilled. Spend today knowing God better. Then tomorrow, you will better know his plans for you.

John 14:1-4 *Don't be troubled. You trust God, now trust in me. There are many rooms in my Father's home, and I am going to prepare a place for you. If this were not so, I would tell you plainly. When everything is ready, I will come and get you, so that you will always be with me where I am. And you know where I am going and how to get there.* When you die, you will go to live with Christ in his home forever.

1 Peter 1:4-5 *For God has reserved a priceless inheritance for his children. It is kept in heaven for you, pure and undefiled, beyond the reach of change and decay. And God, in his mighty power, will protect you until you receive this salvation, because you are trusting him. It will be revealed on the last day for all to see.* You will inherit the heavenly riches reserved for God's children.

Revelation 3:5 *All who are victorious will be clothed in white. I will never erase their names from the Book of Life, but I will announce before my Father*

and his angels that they are mine.
You will wear the garments of heaven and be identified with Christ.

Revelation 21:4 *He will remove all of their sorrows, and there will be no more death or sorrow or crying or pain. For the old world and its evils are gone forever.*
In heaven you will never hurt, cry, have pain, or experience sorrow. Evil will be gone forever.

Colossians 3:4 *And when Christ, who is your real life, is revealed to the whole world, you will share in all his glory.*
You will share the glory that belongs to Christ.

Isaiah 11:6-9 *In that day the wolf and the lamb will live together; the leopard and the goat will be at peace. Calves and yearlings will be safe among lions, and a little child will lead them all. The cattle will graze among bears. Cubs and calves will lie down together. And lions will eat grass as the livestock do. Babies will crawl safely among poisonous snakes. Yes, a little child will put its hand in a nest of deadly snakes and pull it out unharmed. Nothing will hurt or destroy in all my holy mountain. And as the waters fill the sea, so the earth will be filled with people who know the Lord.*

Zechariah 14:9 *And the Lord will be king over all the earth. On that day there will be one Lord— his name alone will be worshiped.*

You will be part of an eternal kingdom ruled by the Lord God himself. It will be free from God's enemies.

1 Thessalonians 5:10 *He died for us so that we can live with him forever, whether we are dead or alive at the time of his return.*
When you die, you will live forever with Christ in heaven.

Acts 1:11 *They said, "Men of Galilee, why are you standing here staring at the sky? Jesus has been taken away from you into heaven. And someday, just as you saw him go, he will return!"*
Some day in the future you will see Christ return again to earth.

Isaiah 25:7-8 *In that day he will remove the cloud of gloom, the shadow of death that hangs over the earth. He will swallow up death forever! The Sovereign Lord will wipe away all tears. He will remove forever all insults and mockery against his land and people. The Lord has spoken!*

Hebrews 2:14 *Because God's children are human beings—made of flesh and blood—Jesus also became flesh and blood by being born in human form. For only as a human being could he die, and only by dying could he break the power of the Devil, who had the power of death.*
Christ will break the power of death and of Satan.

138

How can hope for the future help me live today?

Romans 8:18, 21, 23-25 Yet what we suffer now is nothing compared to the glory he will give us later. . . . All creation anticipates the day when it will join God's children in glorious freedom from death and decay. . . . We, too, wait anxiously for that day when God will give us our full rights as his children, including the new bodies he has promised us. Now that we are saved, we eagerly look forward to this freedom. For if you already have something, you don't need to hope for it. But if we look forward to something we don't have yet, we must wait patiently and confidently.

1 Peter 1:7 These trials are only to test your faith, to show that it is strong and pure. It is being tested as fire tests and purifies gold—and your faith is far more precious to God than mere gold. So if your faith remains strong after being tried by fiery trials, it will bring you much praise and glory and honor on the day when Jesus Christ is revealed to the whole world.

1 Peter 4:13 Instead, be very glad—because these trials will make you partners with Christ in his suffering, and afterward you will have the wonderful joy of sharing his glory when it is displayed to all the world.

1 Thessalonians 4:16-18 For the Lord himself will come down from heaven with a *commanding shout, with the call of the archangel, and with the trumpet call of God. First, all the Christians who have died will rise from their graves. Then, together with them, we who are still alive and remain on the earth will be caught up in the clouds to meet the Lord in the air and remain with him forever. So comfort and encourage each other with these words.*

Philippians 3:13 *No, dear brothers and sisters, I am still not all I should be, but I am focusing all my energies on this one thing: Forgetting the past and looking forward to what lies ahead.*

As a heaven-bound follower of Jesus, you need to put heaven and earth in perspective. Here, we generally live for a hundred years or less. There, 100 million years is just the beginning. If you will spend most of your time in heaven, you need to spend time here preparing yourself to live there. This eternal perspective helps you live here on earth with the right priorities, for this life is really your preparation for life in heaven.

PROMISES FROM GOD: Psalm 32:8 *The Lord says, "I will guide you along the best pathway for your life. I will advise you and watch over you."*

Matthew 26:64 *And in the future you will see me, the Son of Man, sitting at God's right hand in the place of power and coming back on the clouds of heaven.*

Grace

Where does grace come from? How do I receive it?

Psalm 84:11 *He gives us grace and glory. No good thing will the Lord withhold from those who do what is right.*

Grace begins with God and is given freely by God. His graciousness to you is your example for extending grace and mercy to others. Grace cannot be earned. It is freely given.

Ephesians 2:8 *God saved you by his special favor when you believed.*

It is by God's grace that he decided to offer the gift of salvation. There is nothing you can do to earn it. You simply receive it with faith and thankfulness.

Hebrews 4:16 *So let us come boldly to the throne of our gracious God. There we will receive his mercy, and we will find grace to help us when we need it.*

You may freely enter into God's presence where he will freely give his mercy and grace.

PROMISE FROM GOD: Psalm 103:8 *The Lord is merciful and gracious; he is slow to get angry and full of unfailing love.*

Grief

How do I get over my grief?

2 Samuel 18:33 *The king was overcome with emotion. He went up to his room over the gateway and burst into tears. And as he went, he cried, "O my son Absalom!"*

Recognize that grief is necessary and important. You need the freedom to grieve. It is an important part of closure because it allows you to honestly express the way you feel. Grief releases the emotional pressures of sorrow that come from loss.

Genesis 23:2-4 *There Abraham mourned and wept for her. Then, leaving her body, he went to the Hittite elders and said, ". . . Please let me have a piece of land for a burial plot."*

Participate in the process of grief. Take time to personally mourn, but also become involved in the necessary steps to bring closure to your loss. We grieve because we have had a positive experience—what we lost was important to us. Getting involved in the process of grief is a way of honoring what was meaningful.

Ecclesiastes 3:4 *A time to cry and a time to laugh. A time to grieve and a time to dance.*

Grief has its season, and its season may last a

long while. But eventually God will lead you to move on and comfort others who grieve.

2 Corinthians 1:3 *He is the source of every mercy and the God who comforts us.*
God knows we grieve, understands our sorrow, and comforts us. He does not promise to preserve us from grief, but to help us through it.

Revelation 21:4 *He will remove all of their sorrows, and there will be no more death or sorrow or crying or pain.*
Take hope that there will be no more grief in heaven.

In what ways do we grieve?

Nehemiah 2:2-3 *So the king asked me, "Why are you so sad?". . . I replied, ". . . The city where my ancestors are buried is in ruins, and the gates have been burned down."*
We grieve when we see loved ones hurt or in great need.

John 11:35 *Then Jesus wept.*

Acts 9:39 *The room was filled with widows who were weeping.*
We grieve over the death of a loved one.

2 Corinthians 7:10 *For God can use sorrow in our lives to help us turn away from sin and seek salvation.*
We grieve over our sin. It is right to genuinely

143

grieve for our sins and beg God to remove them. Until Christ has cleansed us of those sins, we nurture them and they continue to lurk within us. Confession and forgiveness will cleanse sin and wipe away the tears caused by unconfessed sin.

Luke 13:34 *O Jerusalem, Jerusalem. . . . How often I have wanted to gather your children together as a hen protects her chicks.*
When our hearts are in tune with God's heart, we grieve over lost souls.

PROMISE FROM GOD: Psalm 147:3 *He heals the brokenhearted, binding up their wounds.*

Guilt

(*see also* FORGIVENESS)

How can I be freed from guilt?
Psalm 19:12-13 *Cleanse me from these hidden faults. Keep me from deliberate sins! Don't let them control me. Then I will be free of guilt.*
You can be freed from guilt by avoiding sin as much as possible and confessing any sin to God. Guilt is the consequence of wrongdoing.

Acts 13:39 *Everyone who believes in him is freed from all guilt and declared right with God.*

This is a wonderful example of the grace of God. All you must do is accept God's free gift of salvation. This means believing that God sent his Son, Jesus, to die for your sins so that you are no longer guilty for them.

Jeremiah 3:13 *Only acknowledge your guilt. Admit that you rebelled against the Lord your God.* There is a high cost to acknowledging guilt and admitting sin, but an even higher cost if you don't.

1 John 1:9 *If we confess our sins to him, he is faithful and just to forgive us and to cleanse us from every wrong.* Prayer and confession free you from guilt. Don't let guilty feelings from sin keep you from prayer, because prayer is your only means of confessing to God and restoring your relationship with him.

PROMISE FROM GOD: Romans 8:1 *So now there is no condemnation for those who belong to Christ Jesus.*

Handicapped

Does God care about handicapped people?

Jeremiah 31:8 *For I will bring them from the north and from the distant corners of the earth. I will* not forget the blind and lame, the expectant mothers about to give birth. A great company will return. God's compassionate purposes have always included the handicapped. God loves every person equally regardless of limitations.

Luke 7:22 *Then he told John's disciples, "Go back and tell him what you have seen and heard—the blind see, the lame walk, the lepers are cured, the deaf hear, the dead are raised to life, and the Good News is being preached to the poor."*
Throughout his earthly ministry, Jesus demonstrated special concern for those with handicaps. Jesus' concern for handicapped people did not stay in his heart, but reached out with help and healing.

Isaiah 35:5-6 *And when he comes, he will open the eyes of the blind and unstop the ears of the deaf. The lame will leap like a deer, and those who cannot speak will shout and sing!*
When Jesus returns and the earth is made perfect, all handicaps will be healed.

Can God use handicapped people?

Galatians 6:11 *Notice what large letters I use as I write these closing words in my own handwriting.*
The apostle Paul may have had a serious vision problem, yet the Lord was pleased to use him in mighty ways. We must never use our limitations as an excuse not to serve God.

1 Corinthians 12:7 *A spiritual gift is given to each of us as a means of helping the entire church.* God has given every Christian—including those with handicaps—a spiritual gift for serving others.

PROMISE FROM GOD: Ezekiel 34:15-16 *I myself will tend my sheep and cause them to lie down in peace, says the Sovereign Lord. . . . I will bind up the injured and strengthen the weak.*

Hatred

(*see also* BITTERNESS or FORGIVENESS)

Is it ever appropriate to hate anyone or anything?

Psalm 97:10 *You who love the Lord, hate evil!*

1 John 3:15 *Anyone who hates another Christian is really a murderer at heart.*

Matthew 5:43-44 *You have heard that the law of Moses says, "Love your neighbor" and hate your enemy. But I say, love your enemies!*
We are to love all people and hate all sin. When we truly love God, we will hate sin, because sin separates us from God and damages our relationship with him and with others. Hatred is sin that threatens our very eternal souls. Are you drifting into a love for sinful things? This may be an indicator of a declining love for God.

147

What causes unhealthy hatred?

Galatians 5:19, 22 *When you follow the desires of your sinful nature, your lives will produce these evil results. . . . But when the Holy Spirit controls our lives, he will produce . . . fruit in us.*

Hatred comes from following our own sinful desires. Instead, we must allow the Holy Spirit to fill our lives, leaving no room for hatred.

How do I let go of hatred?

Proverbs 15:1 *A gentle answer turns away wrath, but harsh words stir up anger.*

Get rid of anger. Anger leads to bitterness, which leads to hatred.

Micah 6:8 *This is what he requires: to do what is right, to love mercy, and to walk humbly with your God.*

Mercy and humility are powerful weapons against hatred.

Ephesians 4:31-32 *Get rid of all bitterness. . . . Instead, be kind to each other, tenderhearted, forgiving one another.*

Forgiveness stops hatred.

1 John 4:20 *If someone says, "I love God," but hates a Christian brother or sister, that person is a liar; for if we don't love people we can see, how can we love God, whom we have not seen?*

Genuinely nurturing your love for God will

increase your love for others, and that love will conquer hatred.

What can I do if someone hates me?

Matthew 5:23-24 *If you are standing before the altar in the Temple, offering a sacrifice to God, and you suddenly remember that someone has something against you, leave your sacrifice there beside the altar. Go and be reconciled to that person. Then come and offer your sacrifice to God.*

Examine yourself honestly, searching for anything you have said or done that might have made the other person angry. If there is something, confess it to the other person and ask forgiveness.

Romans 12:20 *If your enemies are hungry, feed them. If they are thirsty, give them something to drink, and they will be ashamed of what they have done to you.*

Continue to act in a loving way toward someone who has hurt you with hatred—but without subjecting yourself to being harmed further. This may influence the other person to change his or her attitude toward you.

PROMISE FROM GOD: Ezekiel 26:26 *And I will give you a new heart with new and right desires, and I will put a new spirit in you. I will take out your stony heart of sin and give you a new, obedient heart.*

Healing

How does God heal?

2 Kings 20:7 *"Make an ointment from figs and spread it over the boil." They did this, and Hezekiah recovered!*
Through physicians and medicine.

Mark 3:5 *Then he said to the man, "Reach out your hand." The man reached out his hand, and it became normal again!*

Luke 5:12-13 *"Lord," he said, "if you want to, you can make me well again." Jesus reached out and touched the man. "I want to," he said. "Be healed!"*
Through miracles.

Mark 2:4-5 *They couldn't get to Jesus through the crowd, so they dug through the clay roof above his head. . . . Seeing their faith, Jesus said to the paralyzed man, "My son, your sins are forgiven."*
Through the faith of friends.

James 5:14 *Are any among you sick? They should call for the elders of the church and have them pray over them.*
Through prayer.

Isaiah 53:5 *He was wounded and crushed for our sins. He was beaten that we might have peace. He was whipped, and we were healed!*
By death Christ brought us life. Through wound-

edness he brought us healing. By accepting our punishment he set us free.

Why doesn't God always heal people?

2 Corinthians 12:9 *My power works best in your weakness.*
We do not know why God heals some people and not others. But we do know that God's power is magnified through our weaknesses and infirmities if we allow him to work within us.

How do I deal with it when I'm not healed?

2 Corinthians 12:10 *Since I know it is all for Christ's good, I am quite content with my weaknesses.*
You can look forward to having God's power work through you in a special way despite your weaknesses. When God works through your weaknesses, it is obvious that what occurred happened because of him, thus showing the world his love and power.

PROMISES FROM GOD: Psalm 147:3 *He heals the brokenhearted, binding up their wounds.*

Malachi 4:2 *But for you who fear my name, the Sun of righteousness will rise with healing in his wings. And you will go free, leaping with joy like calves let out to pasture.*

Heaven

(*see also* SALVATION or VICTORY)

Is there really a heaven?

Genesis 14:22 *Abram replied, "I have solemnly promised the Lord, God Most High, Creator of heaven and earth . . ."*

John 14:2 *There are many rooms in my Father's home, and I am going to prepare a place for you. If this were not so, I would tell you plainly.*

2 Corinthians 5:1 *For we know that when this earthly tent we live in is taken down—when we die and leave these bodies—we will have a home in heaven.* Not only is there a heaven, but Jesus is preparing it for our arrival.

What is heaven like?

Isaiah 65:17 *Look! I am creating new heavens and a new earth—so wonderful that no one will even think about the old ones anymore.*

Philippians 3:21 *He will take these weak mortal bodies of ours and change them into glorious bodies like his own.*

Revelation 22:5 *And there will be no night there—no need for lamps or sun—for the Lord God will shine on them. And they will reign forever and ever.*
Heaven is far beyond anything we can imagine.

There will be no sadness, no pain, no evil, no death. Everything will be perfect and glorious. God will give us new bodies and we will be able to talk face to face with the Lord himself.

How can I be sure I will go to heaven?

John 3:16 *For God so loved the world that he gave his only Son, so that everyone who believes in him will not perish but have eternal life.*

If you have accepted Jesus Christ as Savior and recognize that only he can forgive your sins, you will gain entrance into heaven. You cannot earn your way to heaven, nor is it worth it even to try. Heaven is God's gift to those who trust in Jesus.

PROMISE FROM GOD: 1 Corinthians 2:9 *No eye has seen, no ear has heard, and no mind has imagined what God has prepared for those who love him.*

Helplessness

(*see also* STRENGTH)

What can I do when I feel helpless?

Hebrews 13:6 *The Lord is my helper, so I will not be afraid. What can mere mortals do to me?*

Meditate on God's limitless power and steadfast love for you, reminding yourself that the Lord is far greater than any problem confronting you.

Psalm 18:6 *But in my distress I cried out to the Lord; yes, I prayed to my God for help. He heard me from his sanctuary; my cry reached his ears.*
Pray consistently and confidently for God's help.

Deuteronomy 24:18 *Always remember that you were slaves in Egypt and that the Lord your God redeemed you.*
Take time to reflect on past situations when you felt helpless but the Lord helped you. God's track record in your life can increase your confidence today.

PROMISE FROM GOD: Psalm 118:7 *Yes, the Lord is for me; he will help me.*

Hope

Where does hope come from?

Psalm 71:5 *O Lord, you alone are my hope. I've trusted you, O Lord, from childhood.*
The Lord himself is the source of hope because his character is unchanging, his love is steadfast, his promises will all come true, and his omnipotence determines our future.

Why should I trust God as my hope?

Hebrews 6:18-19 *God has given us both his promise and his oath. These two things are unchangeable because it is impossible for God to lie. Therefore, we who have fled to him for refuge can take new courage, for we can hold on to his promise with confidence. This confidence is like a strong and trustworthy anchor for our souls. It leads us through the curtain of heaven into God's inner sanctuary.*

1 Peter 1:21 *Through Christ you have come to trust in God. And because God raised Christ from the dead and gave him great glory, your faith and hope can be placed confidently in God.*

God cannot lie because he *is* truth. God, therefore, cannot break his promises. His Word stands forever. God must be trusted for your hope because he alone conquered death by raising Christ from the dead.

How can I keep hoping when God never seems to act?

Romans 8:24-25 *For if you already have something, you don't need to hope for it. But if we look forward to something we don't have yet, we must wait patiently and confidently.*

Hope, by definition, is expecting something that has not yet occurred. Once hope is fulfilled, it isn't hope anymore. Thus the practical outworking of hope is patience.

Where can I go to strengthen my hope?

Romans 15:4 *Such things were written in the Scriptures long ago to teach us. They give us hope and encouragement as we wait patiently for God's promises.*

Psalm 119:81, 114 *I faint with longing for your salvation; but I have put my hope in your word. . . . You are my refuge and my shield; your word is my only source of hope.*

Each day you can visit God's Word and have your hope renewed and reinforced. His Word never fails or wavers.

What can I do when things seem hopeless?

1 Samuel 1:10 *Hannah was in deep anguish, crying bitterly as she prayed to the Lord.*

You can pray. In the midst of Hannah's hopelessness, she prayed to God, knowing that if any hope were to be found, it would be found in him.

Acts 16:24-25 *He took no chances but put them into the inner dungeon and clamped their feet in the stocks. Around midnight, Paul and Silas were praying and singing hymns to God.*

You can worship. Paul and Silas were on death row for preaching about Jesus, yet in this hopeless situation they sang praises to God. This reinforced an eternal perspective.

Psalm 27:14 *Wait patiently for the Lord. Be brave and courageous.*

You can remember that God's timing is perfect.

Psalm 18:4-6 *The ropes of death surrounded me; the floods of destruction swept over me. The grave wrapped its ropes around me; death itself stared me in the face. But in my distress I cried out to the Lord; yes, I prayed to my God for help. He heard me from his sanctuary; my cry reached his ears.*

You can remember that sin and evil may sometimes thwart your plans here on earth but cannot affect God's plans in heaven.

PROMISE FROM GOD: Psalm 130:7 *Hope in the Lord; for with the Lord there is unfailing love and an overflowing supply of salvation.*

Insignificance

How can I cope with feelings of insignificance?

Psalm 8:4-5 *What are mortals that you should think of us, mere humans that you should care for us? For you made us only a little lower than God, and you crowned us with glory and honor.*

The Creator of the universe considers you significant.

Matthew 10:29-31 *Not even a sparrow, worth only half a penny, can fall to the ground without your Father knowing it. And the very hairs on your head are all numbered. So don't be afraid; you are more valuable to him than a whole flock of sparrows.*

You matter to God. God thinks every event and detail of your life is important.

Do I have to be "important" for God to use me?

1 Corinthians 1:26-29 *Remember, dear brothers and sisters, that few of you were wise in the world's eyes, or powerful, or wealthy when God called you. Instead, God deliberately chose things the world considers foolish in order to shame those who think they are wise. And he chose those who are powerless to shame those who are powerful. God chose things despised by the world, things counted as nothing at all, and used them to bring to nothing what the world considers important, so that no one can ever boast in the presence of God.*

Significance in the eyes of the world may be insignificance in God's eyes. Insignificance in the world's eyes may be significance in God's eyes. God takes joy in using people the world considers insignificant to accomplish significant things for his kingdom.

Sometimes I look at the successes of the world and feel like my life is completely insignificant. Does my life really matter to God?

Exodus 3:11 *"But who am I to appear before Pharaoh?" Moses asked God.*

Moses offered every excuse in the book for why

he was too insignificant to do God's work, but God saw great potential in him. Don't prevent God from working through you to accomplish great things. God can transform your insecurities into his accomplishments.

Esther 4:16 *And then, though it is against the law, I will go in to see the king. If I must die, I am willing to die.*
Esther was only a young Jewish girl, but God brought her to a position of great influence in order to save her people. God uses even those with insignificant beginnings to fulfill his purpose and plan and bring significant conclusions.

PROMISE FROM GOD: Psalm 8:5 *For you made us only a little lower than God, and you crowned us with glory and honor.*

Intercession

(*see also* PRAYER)

Does it really make a difference when others are praying for me or I am praying for others?

2 Corinthians 1:11 *He will rescue us because you are helping by praying for us.*
Paul was convinced that the Corinthians' prayers were vitally connected to his deliverance by God. Intercession is the practice of praying for the

needs of others. It is easy to become discouraged if you think there is nothing anyone can do for you—or nothing that you can do to help someone you care about. But in fact the most important thing you can do for others, and others can do for you, is to pray. In ways beyond our understanding, intercessory prayer is a channel for the love and power of God, as well as creating a deep bond of fellowship between human beings. Thus intercession is a vital source of hope.

A c t s   1 2 : 5 *But while Peter was in prison, the church prayed very earnestly for him.*
Even as the believers were holding an all-night prayer meeting, God sent an angel to rescue Peter from prison.

What can I ask for when I'm interceding for someone?

3   J o h n   2 *Dear friend, I am praying that all is well with you and that your body is as healthy as I know your soul is.*
You can pray for the person's everyday, practical needs.

1   S a m u e l   1 : 1 7 *May the God of Israel grant the request you have asked of him.*
You can pray that God will satisfy the deepest longings of the person's heart.

E p h e s i a n s   3 : 1 4 - 1 6 *When I think of the wisdom and scope of God's plan, I fall to my knees and pray to the Father, the Creator of everything in heaven and on earth. I pray that from his glorious, unlimited resources he will give you mighty inner strength through his Holy Spirit.*

You can pray for the person's spiritual growth and strength.

PROMISE FROM GOD: James 5:16
The earnest prayer of a righteous person has great power and wonderful results.

Joy

Does God promise me happiness?

James 1:2 *Whenever trouble comes your way, let it be an opportunity for joy.*

God does not promise temporary happiness; in fact the Bible assumes problems will come your way. But God does promise lasting joy for all those who believe in him. This kind of joy stays with you despite your problems. You can have lasting joy even if you don't have temporary happiness.

How can I become more joyful?

Psalm 112:1 *Happy are those who fear the Lord. Yes, happy are those who delight in doing what he commands.*

Fear God and trust in him; delight in doing his commands.

Psalm 16:8-9 *I know the Lord is always with me. . . . No wonder my heart is filled with joy.*
Joy comes from God's presence with you and within you, which brings true contentment.

Galatians 5:22 *But when the Holy Spirit controls our lives, he will produce this kind of fruit in us: love, joy . . .*
The presence of the Holy Spirit in your life produces joy.

Psalm 119:2 *Happy are those who obey his decrees and search for him with all their hearts.*

Philippians 1:25 *I will continue with you so that you will grow and experience the joy of your faith.*
God has promised that when you truly seek him, you will surely find him, and when you find him, your joy is complete.

How can I be joyful in the midst of difficult circumstances?

2 Corinthians 12:10 *Since I know it is all for Christ's good, I am quite content with my weaknesses and with insults, hardships, persecutions, and calamities. For when I am weak, then I am strong.*

1 Peter 4:12-13 *Dear friends, don't be surprised at the fiery trials you are going through, as if something strange were happening to you. Instead, be very glad—because . . . you will have the wonderful joy of sharing his glory.*
Difficult circumstances help you better under-

stand what Christ went through for you. They make you partners with him.

Acts 5:41 *The apostles left the high council rejoicing that God had counted them worthy to suffer dishonor for the name of Jesus.*

Doing something significant for God, even though you may suffer for it, brings great joy because you know that God is working through you to accomplish something important for his Kingdom. You experience joy when you know that God is pleased with you and that your work for him will bring a reward in heaven.

Is it possible to be joyful when I have nothing materially?

Matthew 6:19-21 *Don't store up treasures here on earth, where they can be eaten by moths and get rusty, and where thieves break in and steal. Store your treasures in heaven, where they will never become moth-eaten or rusty and where they will be safe from thieves. Wherever your treasure is, there your heart and thoughts will also be.*

Wherever your money goes, your heart will follow after it. If you spend most of your money collecting something, you become very interested and knowledgeable about what you are collecting. If you spend a lot of your money helping those in need, you become interested and focused on helping the needy. And when you invest in the lives of others, you are investing in eternal treasure.

PROMISE FROM GOD: Nehemiah 8:10 *The joy of the Lord is your strength!*

Justice

Is God always fair and just?

2 Thessalonians 1:5-6 *But God will use this persecution to show his justice, . . . and in his justice he will punish those who persecute you.*
When you are burdened with troubles, it is tempting to think that God is not fair or just. How can God allow a Christian to suffer when so many unbelievers down the street are prospering? But rest assured that God's justice will eventually prevail.

Ezra 9:15 *O Lord, God of Israel, you are just. We stand before you in our guilt.*
We must beg God not for justice, lest he punish us, but for pity, so he will forgive us. We must beg God not for fairness, lest that bring judgment, but for mercy instead.

How do God's justice and mercy relate?

2 Samuel 24:14 *Let us fall into the hands of the Lord, for his mercy is great.*

Romans 6:23 *For the wages of sin is death, but the great gift of God is eternal life through Christ Jesus our Lord.*

God is just in that he very clearly tells us what sin is and what the consequences will be. All people are treated equally. God is merciful in that he offers a way for us to be spared the punishment we deserve for our sin. We would be in much worse shape if we always got the justice we deserved. Justice is getting what we deserve. Mercy is not getting what we deserve. Grace is getting what we do not deserve.

The world seems so unjust. Will God's justice really prevail?

Psalm 96:12-13 *Let the trees of the forest rustle with praise before the Lord! For the Lord is coming! He is coming to judge the earth. He will judge the world with righteousness, and the nations with his truth.*

Complete justice will occur only when Jesus returns as Judge. But make no mistake: This is his solemn promise and it is certain.

How can I work effectively for justice?

Amos 5:21, 24 *I hate all your show and pretense—the hypocrisy of your religious festivals and solemn assemblies. . . . Instead, I want to see a mighty flood of justice, a river of righteous living that will never run dry.*

Make justice a top priority for you and your church. God is not honored by a multitude of programs at a church that has no passion for justice.

Psalm 82:3 *Uphold the rights of the oppressed and the destitute.*
Speak out against injustice.

Isaiah 1:17 *Learn to do good. Seek justice. Help the oppressed. Defend the orphan. Fight for the rights of widows.*
Take the initiative as you strive for justice with energy and dedication.

Isaiah 56:1 *"Be just and fair to all," says the Lord. "Do what is right and good."*

Romans 13:7 *Give to everyone what you owe them.*

Psalm 106:3 *Happy are those who deal justly with others and always do what is right.*
Persist in doing what is right. Don't become unjust yourself.

PROMISES FROM GOD: Romans 12:19 *Never avenge yourselves. Leave that to God. For it is written, "I will take vengeance. I will repay those who deserve it," says the Lord.*

2 Thessalonians 1:6 *In his justice he will punish those who persecute you.*

Leadership

How can leaders inspire hope?

Nehemiah 4:20 *When you hear the blast of the trumpet, rush to wherever it is sounding. Then our God will fight for us!*
Leaders inspire hope through their words and their example of confidence in the Lord.

Deuteronomy 7:17-18 *Perhaps you will think to yourselves, "How can we ever conquer these nations that are so much more powerful than we are?" But don't be afraid of them! Just remember what the Lord your God did to Pharaoh and to all the land of Egypt.*
Leaders inspire hope by reminding people of past victories—especially the victories that demonstrated the power and faithfulness of God.

2 Chronicles 32:20 *Then King Hezekiah and the prophet Isaiah . . . cried out in prayer to God in heaven.*
Leaders inspire hope by being men and women of prayer.

Hebrews 2:10 *Through the suffering of Jesus, God made him a perfect leader, one fit to bring them into their salvation.*
Leaders inspire hope by sharing the hardships of their people.

How can I help my leaders do their best?

1 Thessalonians 5:12-13 *Honor those who are your leaders in the Lord's work. . . . Think highly of them and give them your wholehearted love because of their work.*
Encourage them.

Hebrews 13:18-19 *Pray for us. . . . I especially need your prayers right now.*
Pray for them.

2 Samuel 12:1 *So the Lord sent Nathan the prophet to tell David this story.*
Hold them accountable.

I'm discouraged by the poor quality of my leaders. Is there any hope for improvement?

1 Timothy 2:2 *Pray this way for kings and all others who are in authority, so that we can live in peace and quietness, in godliness and all dignity.*
As long as you can pray, you can hope. Pray that God will improve your leaders—or replace them.

Psalm 146:3, 5 *Don't put your confidence in powerful people; there is no help for you there. . . . But happy are those who have the God of Israel as their helper, whose hope is in the Lord their God.*
Don't forget that even the best human leadership is imperfect. God is the only leader who will never fail.

PROMISE FROM GOD: Jeremiah
3:15 *I will give you leaders after my own heart,
who will guide you with knowledge and understanding.*

Leaving/Farewells

(*see also* MOVING)

What will help me say good-bye in a healthy and positive way?

Acts 20:36-38 *When he had finished speaking,
he knelt and prayed with them. They wept aloud as
they embraced him in farewell, sad most of all
because he had said that they would never see him
again.*
Praying together and being open and honest
about the pain of parting are important to
healthy good-byes.

Philemon 7 *I myself have gained much joy and
comfort from your love, my brother, because your
kindness has so often refreshed the hearts of God's
people.*
Before parting, thank people for what they have
meant to you.

Genesis 12:4 *So Abraham departed, as the Lord
had instructed him.*
Seeing God's hand in your circumstances and

following God's call in your life will give you greater security as you say good-bye, even though parting will still not be easy.

A c t s 2 0 : 3 2 *And now I entrust you to God and the word of his grace—his message that is able to build you up and give you an inheritance with all those he has set apart for himself.*
There is great comfort in knowing that God will take care of those to whom you say farewell. God is near to those with whom you are far apart.

PROMISE FROM GOD: M a t t h e w 2 8 : 2 0 *And be sure of this: I am with you always, even to the end of the age.*

Limitations

(*see also* MISTAKES)

I feel as if I have so many limitations. Am I different from most people?
N u m b e r s 1 1 : 1 4 *I can't carry all these people by myself! The load is far too heavy!*
Even the greatest leaders—like Moses—have limitations. Greatness is not freedom from limitations, but victory over them.

1 P e t e r 1 : 2 4 *People are like grass that dies away; their beauty fades as quickly as the beauty of wild-flowers. The grass withers, and the flowers fall away.*

We are all limited by our physical frailty and by our mortality. If you were totally free from limitations, you wouldn't be human.

Ecclesiastes 8:7 *Indeed, how can people avoid what they don't know is going to happen?*
None of us can see the future, which places severe limitations on us. That's why it is so important to trust God, who does see the future. The strength of God's nature helps you overcome your weaknesses and limitations.

Romans 7:18 *I know I am rotten through and through so far as my old sinful nature is concerned. No matter which way I turn, I can't make myself do right. I want to, but I can't.*
The weakness of our sinful nature greatly limits every one of us.

Can God use me, even with my limitations?

Galatians 6:11 *Notice what large letters I use as I write these closing words in my own handwriting.*

I Timothy 4:12 *Don't let anyone think less of you because you are young. Be an example to all believers in what you teach, in the way you live, in your love, your faith, and your purity.*
The apostle Paul may have been limited by poor eyesight. Timothy faced challenges because he was young. Yet God used them—and many other biblical heroes—despite their limitations.

And he will use you too, if you move forward in faith.

1 Corinthians 12:7 *A spiritual gift is given to each of us as a means of helping the entire church.* No matter what your limitations may be, God has given you a spiritual gift to use in serving others.

Does God have any limitations?

Numbers 11:23 *The Lord said to Moses, "Is there any limit to my power? Now you will see whether or not my word comes true!"*

Isaiah 40:28 *Have you never heard or understood? Don't you know that the Lord is the everlasting God, the Creator of all the earth? He never grows faint or weary.*
There is no limitation to God's power and strength.

Isaiah 40:28 *No one can measure the depths of his understanding.*
God's knowledge has no limit.

PROMISE FROM GOD: Ephesians 3:20 *Glory be to God! By his mighty power at work within us, he is able to accomplish infinitely more than we would ever dare to ask or hope.*

Loneliness

Does God want me to be lonely?

Genesis 2:18 *And the Lord God said, "It is not good for the man to be alone. I will make a companion who will help him."*

God did not intend for you to be lonely. Quite the contrary; it was God who recognized Adam's need for companionship. He gave Adam the task of naming the animals so that Adam could recognize his own need for a companion. It was then that God created woman.

Romans 8:38-39 *And I am convinced that nothing can ever separate us from his love. Death can't, and life can't. The angels can't, and the demons can't. Our fears for today, our worries about tomorrow, and even the powers of hell can't keep God's love away. Whether we are high above the sky or in the deepest ocean, nothing in all creation will ever be able to separate us from the love of God that is revealed in Christ Jesus our Lord.*

God never intended for you to be alone. He has promised that he will always be with you. Nothing can separate you from him. He intended for you to have a spiritual as well as a human relationship.

How can God help me with my loneliness?

Psalm 139:17 *How precious are your thoughts about me, O God!*

Isaiah 54:10 *For the mountains may depart and the hills disappear, but even then I will remain loyal to you.*
Recognize that you are not unlovable or deficient just because you are lonely. You have value because God made you, loves you, and promises never to leave you.

1 Peter 4:19 *So if you are suffering according to God's will, keep on doing what is right, and trust yourself to the God who made you, for he will never fail you.*
Sometimes you may feel alone in your stand for Christ. You can take comfort in knowing that there are others who are equally committed and that God rewards your bold commitment.

Romans 12:5 *And since we are all one body in Christ, we belong to each other, and each of us needs all the others.*
The best way to avoid loneliness is to get together with other believers. Get involved in a local church. Get busy with God's people doing God's work.

Isaiah 41:10 *Don't be afraid, for I am with you. Do not be dismayed, for I am your God. I will strengthen you. I will help you. I will uphold you with my victorious right hand.*

John 14:1 *Don't be troubled. You trust God, now trust in me.*

Loneliness can cause you to be afraid. Trust God and let him calm your fears.

I feel like everyone has deserted me.

Psalm 27:10 *Even if my father and mother abandon me, the Lord will hold me close.*

Proverbs 18:24 *There are "friends" who destroy each other, but a real friend sticks closer than a brother.*

Psalm 147:3 *He heals the brokenhearted, binding up their wounds.*

Hebrews 13:5 *God has said, "I will never fail you. I will never forsake you."*
People we depend on sometimes desert us, abandon us, or turn away from us. There may be only a few people you can truly count on—at times there may not be any. But you can always count on God; he will never abandon you.

How can I help those who are lonely?

3 John 5 *You are doing a good work for God when you take care of the traveling teachers who are passing through.*

James 1:27 *We must care for orphans and widows in their troubles.*
Invite them into your home and befriend them.

PROMISE FROM GOD: Psalm 23:4 *Even when I walk through the dark valley of death, . . . you are close beside me.*

Loss

How do I deal with loss in my life?

John 11:35 *Then Jesus wept.*
Don't deny your loss. Great grief is the result of great love. The tears of Jesus at Lazarus's death forever validate our tears of grief.

Genesis 50:3 *There was a period of national mourning for seventy days.*
Grief is a process that must not be denied or hurried. The rituals of wakes, visitations, funerals, and memorial services all help you move through the stages of grief.

Job 1:20-21 *Job stood up and tore his robe in grief. . . . He said, ". . . The Lord gave me everything I had, and the Lord has taken it away."*
Losses always bring pain. Recognizing and expressing that pain is not wrong or sinful, but is rather a healthy expression of how God created us.

Lamentations 3:19-23 *The thought of my suffering and homelessness is bitter beyond words. I will never forget this awful time, as I grieve over my loss. Yet I still dare to hope when I remember this: The unfailing love of the Lord never ends! By his mercies we have been kept from complete destruction. Great is his faithfulness; his mercies begin afresh each day.*

Believers grieve with God, the source of greatest hope. Unbelievers grieve without God, and therefore have no hope.

I feel like I've lost everything. Where can I turn?

Psalm 31:9-10 *Have mercy on me, Lord, for I am in distress. My sight is blurred because of my tears. My body and soul are withering away. I am dying from grief; my years are shortened by sadness. Misery has drained my strength; I am wasting away from within.*

Psalm 56:8 *You keep track of all my sorrows. You have collected all my tears in your bottle. You have recorded each one in your book.*

Turn to God in times of loss, for he alone can give you hope.

2 Corinthians 1:4 *He comforts us in all our troubles so that we can comfort others. When others are troubled, we will be able to give them the same comfort God has given us.*

Turn to God's people in times of loss, for they can give you God's counsel.

How can God help me survive life's losses?

Psalm 10:17 *Lord, you know the hopes of the helpless. Surely you will listen to their cries and comfort them.*

Psalm 102:17 *He will listen to the prayers of the destitute. He will not reject their pleas.*

Lamentations 3:32 *Though he brings grief, he also shows compassion according to the greatness of his unfailing love.*

Psalm 30:11-12 *You have turned my mourning into joyful dancing. You have taken away my clothes of mourning and clothed me with joy, that I might sing praises to you and not be silent. O Lord my God, I will give you thanks forever!*
In times of loss, God fills you with his blessings—comfort, joy, songs of praise, thanksgiving, and mercy. When you cry out for someone to touch you, God will hold you close.

PROMISE FROM GOD: **Psalm 34:18** *The Lord is close to the brokenhearted; he rescues those who are crushed in spirit.*

Love

I feel unlovable. Does anyone really love me?

Romans 5:8 *But God showed his great love for us by sending Christ to die for us while we were still sinners.*
The death of Jesus proves God's love for you. How much God loves you is measured by how much he was willing to give up for you.

How can I more fully accept God's love?

John 13:8 *"No," Peter protested, "you will never*

wash my feet!" Jesus replied, "But if I don't wash you, you won't belong to me."

You begin to accept God's love when you put aside your pride and self-sufficiency.

Philippians 3:9 *I no longer count on my own goodness or my ability to obey God's law, but I trust Christ to save me.*

When you stop trying to impress God with your accomplishments, you are able to trust and enjoy his gracious gift of love. God embraces you not for how much you have done but for how much you have received his love.

Hosea 2:20 *I will be faithful to you and make you mine, and you will finally know me as Lord.*

Nurturing your relationship with God through worship, Bible reading, and prayer will help you grow more confident in God's faithful love.

Where can I get a true love for others? Where does that come from?

1 Thessalonians 3:12 *And may the Lord make your love grow and overflow to each other and to everyone else, just as our love overflows toward you.*

1 Thessalonians 4:9 *For God himself has taught you to love one another.*

God didn't just create love, he *is* love. Trace love all the way back to its source, and there is God. So when you invite God into your heart, you have the very love of God inside you to show toward others. Unlike God, who has no sinful nature, your sinful nature will always try to extinguish this love. You must learn how to love by constantly keeping your sin nature in check so that your love for others will be clearly seen.

How can I love people I don't even like?

1 John 4:19 *We love each other as a result of his loving us first.*
As you reflect on God's love for you and receive it for yourself, you will grow in your ability to love those you do not like.

Romans 12:20 *If your enemies are hungry, feed them. If they are thirsty, give them something to drink.*
Even if you don't like certain people, you can choose to do tangible acts of love for them.

Matthew 5:43-44 *You have heard that the law of Moses says, "Love your neighbor" and hate your enemy. But I say, love your enemies! Pray for those who persecute you!*
Remember that loving enemies is mandatory for Christians. It is possible only as you follow Jesus' example and are filled with the Holy Spirit's power.

How can I rekindle love in my marriage?

Hebrews 13:4 *Give honor to marriage, and remain faithful to one another in marriage.*
It is essential to reaffirm an irrevocable commit-

ment to stay married. Then when problems
come, you won't be looking for a way out, but
a way through.

Song of Songs 4:1 *How beautiful you are,
my beloved, how beautiful! Your eyes behind your veil
are like doves. Your hair falls in waves, like a flock
of goats frisking down the slopes of Gilead.*
Make it a point to give compliments and affirmation to your spouse every day.

Song of Songs 2:10-13 *My lover said to me,
"Rise up, my beloved, my fair one, and come away.
For the winter is past, and the rain is over and gone.
The flowers are springing up, and the time of singing
birds has come, even the cooing of turtledoves. The fig
trees are budding, and the grapevines are in blossom.
How delicious they smell! Yes, spring is here! Arise,
my beloved, my fair one, and come away."*
Take a break together from responsibilities and
routine. Have fun! Enjoy life and one another!

Proverbs 12:15 *Fools think they need no advice,
but the wise listen to others.*
Don't be afraid to seek the counsel of a pastor
or therapist.

PROMISES FROM GOD:
Psalm 23:6 *Surely your goodness and unfailing
love will pursue me all the days of my life.*

Psalm 103:8 *The Lord is merciful and gracious
. . . full of unfailing love.*

Meaning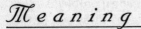

(*see also* FULFILLMENT and PURPOSE)

Why does it sometimes seem that life lacks meaning?

Ecclesiastes 3:19 *For humans and animals both breathe the same air, and both die. So people have no real advantage over the animals. How meaningless!*

The inevitability of death can make life seem meaningless. But the joy of living God's way brings great meaning.

Ecclesiastes 4:4 *Then I observed that most people are motivated to success by their envy of their neighbors. But this, too, is meaningless, like chasing the wind.*

Basing our actions on trivial or selfish motives can make life seem meaningless. We should keep our goals high, but our motives pure.

Ecclesiastes 5:10 *Those who love money will never have enough. How absurd to think that wealth brings true happiness!*

Centering our lives on money and possessions leads to a sense of meaninglessness. Wanting more only causes us to want yet more. With this attitude, there is never enough.

What is life's deepest meaning?

Ezekiel 29:21 *Then they will know that I am the Lord.*

We are created to know God and enjoy fellowship with him.

Psalm 8:3-8 *When I look at the night sky and see the work of your fingers—the moon and the stars you have set in place—what are mortals that you should think of us, mere humans that you should care for us? For you made us only a little lower than God, and you crowned us with glory and honor. You put us in charge of everything you made, giving us authority over all things—the sheep and the cattle and all the wild animals, the birds in the sky, the fish in the sea, and everything that swims the ocean currents.*

God has given humans the highest place in creation and the great responsibility of managing and caring for God's creation. This is a high honor!

Romans 8:29 *For God knew his people in advance, and he chose them to become like his Son, so that his Son would be the firstborn, with many brothers and sisters.*

2 Peter 1:3 *As we know Jesus better, his divine power gives us everything we need for living a godly life. He has called us to receive his own glory and goodness!*

God intends for us to become more and more like the Lord Jesus.

Ephesians 1:5 *His unchanging plan has always been to adopt us into his own family by bringing us to himself through Jesus Christ. And this gave him great pleasure.*
God's purpose for us is to be his children and to live in the complete security of his love every moment.

2 Corinthians 5:18 *All this newness of life is from God, who brought us back to himself through what Christ did. And God has given us the task of reconciling people to himself.*
We are called to participate in God's work in the world and make an eternal impact on others for him.

John 20:21 *He spoke to them again and said, "Peace be with you. As the Father has sent me, so I send you."*
We are called to continue Christ's mission in the world.

John 11:25-26 *Jesus told her, "I am the resurrection and the life. Those who believe in me, even though they die like everyone else, will live again. They are given eternal life for believing in me and will never perish."*
The fact that death is not the end for Jesus' followers invests our lives with eternal significance. Knowing there is life after death gives us true perspective.

How can I understand the meaning of my life more fully?

Proverbs 2:3-4 *Cry out for insight and understanding. Search for them as you would for lost money or hidden treasure.*

Proverbs 4:7 *Getting wisdom is the most important thing you can do!*
Understanding the deep truths of life doesn't just happen. You have to make it a top priority. You won't stumble onto insight, understanding, and wisdom by accident. You find them only when you pursue them.

Psalm 119:104 *Your commandments give me understanding; no wonder I hate every false way of life.*
Studying the Bible will provide greater insight into your life's meaning.

Psalm 57:2 *I cry out to God Most High, to God who will fulfill his purpose for me.*
Make sure to pray, asking God to reveal his truth to you and to fulfill his purpose in you.

PROMISES FROM GOD: Jeremiah 1:4-5 *The Lord gave me a message. He said, "I knew you before I formed you in your mother's womb. Before you were born I set you apart."*

Proverbs 2:6 *For the Lord grants wisdom! From his mouth come knowledge and understanding.*

Miracles

(*see also* HEALING)

What are miracles?

Isaiah 41:19-20 *I will plant trees—cedar, acacia, myrtle, olive, cypress, fir, and pine—on barren land. Everyone will see this miracle and understand that it is the Lord, the Holy One of Israel, who did it.*

Miracles are visible signs that only God can perform. They help us know him and see his hand in our lives.

How does God use miracles?

Daniel 6:27 *He rescues and saves his people; he performs miraculous signs and wonders in the heavens and on earth. He has rescued Daniel from the power of the lions.*

Micah 7:15 *"Yes," says the Lord, "I will do mighty miracles for you, like those I did when I rescued you from slavery in Egypt."*

God uses miracles to rescue us.

Exodus 10:1 *Then the Lord said to Moses, "Return to Pharaoh and again make your demands. I have made him and his officials stubborn so I can continue to display my power by performing miraculous signs among them."*

God uses miracles to show his power.

Matthew 14:14 *A vast crowd was there as he stepped from the boat, and he had compassion on them and healed their sick.*
God uses miracles to show his compassion for us.

What should my response be when God performs miracles in my life?

Luke 19:37 *As they reached the place where the road started down from the Mount of Olives, all of his followers began to shout and sing as they walked along, praising God for all the wonderful miracles they had seen.*
You should offer praise and thanksgiving to him.

Psalm 9:1 *I will thank you, Lord, with all my heart; I will tell of all the marvelous things you have done.*
You can best show your thanks by becoming a testimony to what God has done for you.

Should I be disappointed with God when he doesn't perform a miracle I pray for?

Psalm 107:1 *Give thanks to the Lord, for he is good! His faithful love endures forever.*
We don't know that God will always do miracles, but we do know that God's love for us is eternal and unchanging. You can therefore trust that God is doing a good work in your life even when he doesn't give you exactly what you pray for. The miracle of God's love for sinners is the greatest miracle of all.

PROMISE FROM GOD: Luke 1:37
For nothing is impossible with God.

Mistakes

Is there hope for me, even with all the mistakes I've made?

Jonah 1:3 *But Jonah got up and went in the opposite direction in order to get away from the Lord.*
The worst mistake you can make is running from God, yet God pursued Jonah and gave him another chance.

Exodus 2:12 *After looking around to make sure no one was watching, Moses killed the Egyptian and buried him in the sand.*
Even Moses' life was marred by an immature and terrible mistake.

Matthew 26:74 *Peter said, "I swear by God, I don't know the man."*
Christ restored Peter to fellowship even after his most painful mistake. Following Christ means allowing him to forgive your mistakes and call you to a more glorious future.

How should I respond when I make a mistake?

Genesis 3:12-13 *"Yes," Adam admitted, "but it was the woman you gave me who brought me the fruit, and I ate it.". . . "The serpent tricked me,"* she replied. Take responsibility and don't try to shift the blame.

Philippians 3:13 *No, dear brothers and sisters, I am still not all I should be, but I am focusing all my energies on this one thing: Forgetting the past and looking forward to what lies ahead.*
Don't get stuck dwelling on the past.

John 21:15 *After breakfast Jesus said to Simon Peter, "Simon, son of John, do you love me more than these?" "Yes, Lord," Peter replied, "you know I love you." "Then feed my lambs," Jesus told him.*
Move forward by doing what God has called you to do today.

PROMISE FROM GOD: Romans 8:28 *And we know that God causes everything to work together for the good of those who love God and are called according to his purpose for them.*

Moving

How can I best handle a move?
Psalm 139:3, 5, 7, 9-10 *You chart the path ahead of me and tell me where to stop and rest. Every moment you know where I am. . . . You both precede and follow me. You place your hand of blessing on my head. . . . I can never escape from your spirit! I can*

never get away from your presence! . . . If I dwell by the farthest oceans, even there your hand will guide me, and your strength will support me.

When you move to a new place, you should recognize that God is already there, preparing that place for you and you for that place.

N u m b e r s 9 : 2 1 *Sometimes the cloud stayed only overnight and moved on the next morning. But day or night, when the cloud lifted, the people broke camp and followed.*

When you move to a new place, you must pray for the Lord's presence to be with you at all times.

N u m b e r s 1 0 : 1 3 *When the time to move arrived, the Lord gave the order through Moses.*

You should seek the Lord's direction in each move you make.

G e n e s i s 1 3 : 1 8 *Then Abram moved his camp to the oak grove owned by Mamre, which is at Hebron. There he built an altar to the Lord.*

Throughout any move, you must continue to worship the Lord regularly, for he is the guardian of your move.

How can God help me in my move?

I s a i a h 4 1 : 1 3 *I am holding you by your right hand—I, the Lord your God. And I say to you, "Do not be afraid. I am here to help you."*

E z r a 8 : 2 1 *And there by the Ahava Canal, I gave orders for all of us to fast and humble ourselves before* our God. We prayed that he would give us a safe journey and protect us, our children, and our goods as we traveled.

Exodus 33:14-15 *And the Lord replied, "I will personally go with you, Moses. I will give you rest—everything will be fine for you." Then Moses said, "If you don't go with us personally, don't let us move a step from this place."*
God will guide you, give you wisdom and courage, and be with you wherever your move takes you—if only you ask him.

How do I move forward in my spiritual life?

Philippians 1:6 *And I am sure that God, who began the good work within you, will continue his work until it is finally finished on that day when Christ Jesus comes back again.*

Job 17:9 *The righteous will move onward and forward, and those with pure hearts will become stronger and stronger.*

Romans 12:2 *Don't copy the behavior and customs of this world, but let God transform you into a new person by changing the way you think. Then you will know what God wants you to do, and you will know how good and pleasing and perfect his will really is.*

Ephesians 4:15 *We will hold to the truth in love, becoming more and more in every way like Christ, who is the head of his body, the church.*

God challenges you to move forward toward greater growth and maturity in your relationship with him. Standing still in the Christian life is really moving backward.

PROMISE FROM GOD: Joshua 1:9 *The Lord your God is with you wherever you go.*

Opportunities

How can I make the most of opportunities?

Ephesians 5:16 *Make the most of every opportunity for doing good in these evil days.*

Philippians 1:14 *And because of my imprisonment, many of the Christians here have gained confidence and become more bold in telling others about Christ.*
Seize opportunities to do good, even when you are experiencing personal hardship.

Jeremiah 13:16 *Give glory to the Lord your God before it is too late. Acknowledge him before he brings darkness upon you, causing you to stumble and fall on the dark mountains.*
Respond to God's call and get to know him and his truth, while there is opportunity.

Proverbs 12:11 *Hard work means prosperity; only fools idle away their time.*

John 9:4 *All of us must quickly carry out the tasks assigned us by the one who sent me, because there is little time left before the night falls and all work comes to an end.*
When an opportunity presents itself, respond by acting quickly and working hard.

1 Corinthians 16:8-9 *In the meantime, I will be staying here at Ephesus until the Festival of Pentecost, for there is a wide-open door for a great work here, and many people are responding.*

Acts 11:19 *Meanwhile, the believers who had fled from Jerusalem during the persecution after Stephen's death traveled as far as Phoenicia, Cyprus, and Antioch of Syria. They preached the Good News.*
Use unexpected change or difficulty as an opportunity to serve God.

How do I know if an opportunity is from God?

1 Thessalonians 5:17 *Keep on praying.*
Stay close to God through prayer and ask for his guidance.

Psalm 119:105 *Your word is a lamp for my feet and a light for my path.*
The Bible will not always speak directly in favor of a particular opportunity, but any opportunity that contradicts God's Word or leads you away from its principles is not from the Lord.

Acts 8:30 *Philip ran over and heard the man reading from the prophet Isaiah; so he asked, "Do you understand what you are reading?"*
You should always be ready to seize an opportunity to witness for Christ in word or deed.

Philippians 1:12 *And I want you to know, dear brothers and sisters, that everything that has happened to me here has helped to spread the Good News.*
Christ helps you turn your problems into opportunities.

Deuteronomy 1:28 *How can we go on? Our scouts have demoralized us with their report.*
Fear and doubt can cause you to miss God's opportunities. Opportunities that require faith and courage are often from God.

PROMISE FROM GOD: Revelation 3:8 *I know all the things you do, and I have opened a door for you that no one can shut.*

Oppression

(*see* PERSECUTION or SUFFERING or TROUBLE or PREJUDICE)

What does God think of oppression?
Exodus 22:21 *Do not oppress foreigners in any way.*

Zechariah 7:10 *Do not oppress widows, orphans, foreigners, and poor people.*
God hates oppression and expressly forbids it in any form.

Does God care about oppressed people?

Psalm 72:12 *He will help the oppressed, who have no one to defend them.*
God has a special love for those who are oppressed, and he promises to be with them and help them.

Zephaniah 3:19 *And I will deal severely with all who have oppressed you.*
God promises to judge oppressors.

Luke 1:52 *He has taken princes from their thrones and exalted the lowly.*
When Jesus returns, he will put an end to oppression forever.

What does God call us to do about oppression?

Amos 5:23-24 *Away with your hymns of praise! They are only noise to my ears. I will not listen to your music, no matter how lovely it is. Instead, I want to see a mighty flood of justice, a river of righteous living that will never run dry.*
God urges us to recognize that doing justice is central to godly living. Wonderful worship and pious prayer are exposed as hypocrisy if they are

not accompanied by opposing oppression and aiding the oppressed.

Ezekiel 45:9 *For this is what the Sovereign Lord says: Enough, you princes of Israel! Stop all your violence and oppression and do what is just and right.* We are to refuse to participate in any form of oppression as well as calling those in power to account.

PROMISE FROM GOD: Psalm 9:9 *The Lord is a shelter for the oppressed, a refuge in times of trouble.*

Overcoming

Can I really overcome the obstacles and enemies I face?

John 16:33 *Here on earth you will have many trials and sorrows. But take heart, because I have overcome the world.*
Jesus realistically prepares you for life's problems, yet he also guarantees victory.

1 John 5:4-5 *For every child of God defeats this evil world by trusting Christ to give the victory. And the ones who win this battle against the world are the ones who believe that Jesus is the Son of God.*
You overcome by trusting in Jesus' strength, not your own.

How can I be an overcomer?

2 Corinthians 4:8-9 *We are pressed on every side by troubles, but we are not crushed or broken. We are perplexed, but we don't give up and quit. We are hunted down, but God never abandons us. We get knocked down, but we get up again and keep going.*

With confidence in God's presence, you must develop the ability to endure setbacks without surrendering.

2 Corinthians 4:18 *So we don't look at the troubles we can see right now; rather, we look forward to what we have not yet seen. For the troubles we see will soon be over, but the joys to come will last forever.*

An eternal perspective is an indispensable attribute of the overcomer. Unseen solutions will replace visible problems.

Can I overcome the disadvantages of my birth and the dysfunction of my family of origin?

Judges 11:1-2 *Now Jephthah of Gilead was a great warrior. He was the son of Gilead, but his mother was a prostitute. Gilead's wife also had several sons, and when these half brothers grew up, they chased Jephthah off the land. "You will not get any of our father's inheritance," they said, "for you are the son of a prostitute."*

Despite being scorned and rejected because of his illegitimate birth, Jephthah became a military hero and judge of all Israel.

2 Kings 11:1-3 *When Athaliah, the mother of King Ahaziah of Judah, learned that her son was dead, she set out to destroy the rest of the royal family. But Ahaziah's sister Jehosheba, the daughter of King Jehoram, took Ahaziah's infant son, Joash, and stole him away from among the rest of the king's children, who were about to be killed. Jehosheba put Joash and his nurse in a bedroom to hide him from Athaliah, so the child was not murdered. Joash and his nurse remained hidden in the Temple of the Lord for six years while Athaliah ruled the land.*
Joash was raised in hiding after the rest of his family was murdered, yet he became one of the wisest and most godly kings of Judah.

PROMISES FROM GOD: Romans 8:37 *No, despite all these things, overwhelming victory is ours through Christ, who loved us.*

Philippians 4:13 *For I can do everything with the help of Christ who gives me the strength I need.*

Jeremiah 15:20 *They will fight against you like an attacking army, but I will make you as secure as a fortified wall. They will not conquer you, for I will protect and deliver you. I, the Lord, have spoken!*

Patience

How can I grow in patience?

J a m e s   5 : 7 - 8   *Consider the farmers who eagerly look for the rains in the fall and in the spring. They patiently wait for the precious harvest to ripen.* Whether you're waiting for crops to ripen, a traffic jam to unsnarl, a child to mature, or God to perfect you, you can grow in patience by recognizing that these things take time and there is only so much you can do—if anything—to speed them up. A key to understanding God's will is to understand God's timing.

P s a l m   4 0 : 1   *I waited patiently for the Lord to help me, and he turned to me and heard my cry.*

H a b a k k u k   2 : 3   *If it seems slow, wait patiently, for it will surely take place. It will not be delayed.* You must wait patiently in prayer for God to do his work. Remember that God's plan will be accomplished—but not on your schedule.

G a l a t i a n s   5 : 2 2   *But when the Holy Spirit controls our lives, he will produce this kind of fruit in us: love, joy, peace, patience, . . .* The more you let the Holy Spirit fill you and rule you, the more patient you will become. Fruit growing of all kinds, including the fruit of the Holy Spirit, takes time.

Is patience really worth working for?

Romans 15:5 *May God, who gives this patience and encouragement, help you live in complete harmony with each other—each with the attitude of Christ Jesus toward the other.*

Colossians 1:11 *We also pray that you will be strengthened with his glorious power so that you will have all the patience and endurance you need. May you be filled with joy.*

Patience leads to harmony with others, endurance to handle difficult circumstances, and an expectant attitude of hope that things will get better. It demonstrates a thoughtful and careful attitude toward others' feelings. Anyone can be patient, but there is a higher level of patience that comes from God through his Holy Spirit's presence and work in our lives.

Ephesians 4:2 *Be humble and gentle. Be patient with each other, making allowance for each other's faults because of your love.*

Patience is a characteristic of love. The more loving we become, the more we model the nature of God in our lives. God is incredibly patient. Love requires us to be patient with those we love.

Hebrews 10:36 *Patient endurance is what you need now, so you will continue to do God's will. Then you will receive all that he has promised.*

Patience is evidence of strength of character. Tested faith should grow patient endurance.

Genesis 29:20-21, 25, 27-28 *So Jacob spent the next seven years working to pay for Rachel. But his love for her was so strong that it seemed to him but a few days. Finally, the time came for him to marry her. "I have fulfilled my contract," Jacob said to Laban. "Now give me my wife so we can be married.". . . But when Jacob woke up in the morning—it was Leah! "What sort of trick is this?" Jacob raged at Laban. "I worked seven years for Rachel. What do you mean by this trickery?". . . "Wait until the bridal week is over, and you can have Rachel, too—that is, if you promise to work another seven years for me." So Jacob agreed to work seven more years.*

Patience is the key to achieving many goals. Achieving goals is rarely done with a quantum leap, but rather by small footsteps.

2 Thessalonians 1:4 *We proudly tell God's other churches about your endurance and faithfulness in all the persecutions and hardships you are suffering.*

Patience is the key to enduring suffering. Suffering is better endured when patiently endured.

Exodus 32:1 *When Moses failed to come back down the mountain right away, the people went to Aaron. "Look," they said, "make us some gods who can lead us. This man Moses, who brought us here from Egypt, has disappeared. We don't know what has happened to him."*

Impatience can lead to poor life choices.

What does it mean to "wait on the Lord"?

Isaiah 33:2 *But Lord, be merciful to us, for we have waited for you. Be our strength each day and our salvation in times of trouble.*

Isaiah 40:31 *But those who wait on the Lord will find new strength. They will fly high on wings like eagles. They will run and not grow weary. They will walk and not faint.*

Isaiah 8:17 *I will wait for the Lord to help us, though he has turned away from the people of Israel. My only hope is in him.*

Waiting on the Lord is bringing our timetable in sync with his. We try not to rush ahead of him or linger too far behind him. Waiting on the Lord is relying on him as the source of our daily strength for all situations, realizing our total dependence on him, and maintaining our hope in the promises of his Word.

PROMISE FROM GOD: Lamentations 3:25 *The Lord is wonderfully good to those who wait for him and seek him.*

Peace

Where can I find peace?

Psalm 4:8 *I will lie down in peace and sleep, for you alone, O Lord, will keep me safe.*

Psalm 29:11 *The Lord gives his people strength. The Lord blesses them with peace.*
Peace from the chaos of the world will only come when you have entered heaven for all eternity. But peace of mind and heart come from inviting God—the true source of peace—to dwell in you, helping you to understand that this world is only temporary. Then you can navigate through any chaos because you know God is ultimately in control.

How can I get inner peace?

Romans 2:10 *But there will be glory and honor and peace from God for all who do good.*
Turn from sin to God and live a life of obedience.

Isaiah 26:3 *You will keep in perfect peace all who trust in you, whose thoughts are fixed on you!*
Choose to focus on the Lord more than on your problems.

Galatians 5:22 *But when the Holy Spirit controls our lives, he will produce this kind of fruit in us: . . . peace . . .*
Let the Holy Spirit fill and rule your life.

Philippians 4:6-7 *Don't worry about anything; instead, pray about everything. Tell God what you need, and thank him for all he has done. If you do this, you will experience God's peace, which is far more wonderful than the human mind can understand. His peace will guard your hearts and minds as you live in Christ Jesus.*
Pray about everything. Prayer is indispensable to inner peace.

How can I make peace with others?

Psalm 34:14 *Work hard at living in peace with others.*
Remember that peaceful relationships don't just happen; they take work.

Matthew 18:15 *If another believer sins against you, go privately and point out the fault. If the other person listens and confesses it, you have won that person back.*
True peace does not come when you try to avoid all conflict. Honestly confronting problems in a relationship is necessary for genuine harmony.

Ephesians 4:3 *Always keep yourselves united in the Holy Spirit, and bind yourselves together with peace.*
Seek the unity that comes from the Holy Spirit.

Romans 12:17-18 *Never pay back evil for evil to anyone. . . . Do your part to live in peace with everyone.*

Through genuine forgiveness, rid your life of revenge—not only the retaliatory actions, but also the feelings and fantasies.

Is there any hope for world peace?

Micah 4:3 *The Lord will settle international disputes. All the nations will beat their swords into plowshares and their spears into pruning hooks. All wars will stop, and military training will come to an end.*

War is an inevitable consequence of human sin. But when Jesus returns, there will be peace.

PROMISE FROM GOD: John 14:27 *I am leaving you with a gift—peace of mind and heart.*

Persecution

(*see also* SUFFERING)

Why are Christians persecuted?

John 15:21 *The people of the world will hate you because you belong to me, for they don't know God who sent me.*

Sometimes believers are persecuted simply for speaking the truth. Those who don't believe in God, or don't believe God has established absolute truths and communicated them through the Bible, obviously don't recognize truth. To them, truth sounds rigid and intolerant. Others recognize the truth but don't want to live by it. In either case, those who don't live by the truths of the Bible will persecute those who do.

GALATIANS 5:11 *The fact that I am still being persecuted proves that I am still preaching salvation.* The bold message of Christ threatens those who believe in their own righteousness.

Where can I find hope when I am persecuted?

2 TIMOTHY 3:12 *Yes, and everyone who wants to live a godly life in Christ Jesus will suffer persecution.* You can be encouraged by the fact that persecution is often the norm, not the exception, for faithful Christian disciples.

1 PETER 4:13 *Instead, be very glad—because these trials will make you partners with Christ in his suffering, and afterward you will have the wonderful joy of sharing his glory.*

ACTS 5:41 *The apostles left the high council rejoicing that God had counted them worthy to suffer dishonor for the name of Jesus.*
The Bible encourages you to see persecution for Jesus' sake as an honor. It is evidence of the depth of your commitment to Jesus and therefore a privilege to suffer for the God you love so much.

It also acknowledges the depth of suffering Jesus went through for us.

How are Christians to respond to persecution?

Matthew 5:44 *But I say, love your enemies! Pray for those who persecute you!*

Romans 12:14 *If people persecute you because you are a Christian, don't curse them; pray that God will bless them.*
We are to pray that God will bless those who persecute us, for it may be through our godly response to their persecution that God touches a hard heart and turns it to him.

Revelation 14:12 *Let this encourage God's holy people to endure persecution patiently and remain firm to the end, obeying his commands and trusting in Jesus.*

Matthew 27:12 *But when the leading priests and other leaders made their accusations against him, Jesus remained silent.*
We are to remain obedient to God and endure the persecution patiently, just as Jesus did when he was persecuted.

PROMISE FROM GOD: Revelation 2:10 *Don't be afraid of what you are about to suffer. . . . Remain faithful even when facing death, and I will give you the crown of life.*

Perseverance

How do I develop perseverance in my life?

Joshua 6:3 *Your entire army is to march around the city once a day for six days.*

Perseverance is obeying God even when his way doesn't seem to make sense or produce immediate results.

Romans 5:3 *We can rejoice, too, when we run into problems and trials, for we know that they are good for us.*

When you see the potential that suffering has to produce character in your life, you persevere through it with God's help.

Revelation 14:12 *Let this encourage God's holy people to endure persecution patiently.*

The key to perseverance is having a clear view of the goal of heaven. When you see clearly where you are going, you can endure the hardships along the road.

If I am saved by grace and not by works, where does persevering in following Jesus come in?

2 Peter 1:6 *Patient endurance leads to godliness.*

Through patient perseverance, you become more like Jesus.

James 1:3 *For when your faith is tested, your endurance has a chance to grow.*

208

Perseverance turns suffering into maturity. Suffering for the sake of suffering is fruitless. But suffering that leads to maturity is productive.

PROMISE FROM GOD: Matthew 7 : 7 *Keep on asking, and you will be given what you ask for. Keep on looking, and you will find. Keep on knocking, and the door will be opened.*

Persistence

How is persistence an important character quality?

Genesis 18:32 *Finally, Abraham said, "Lord, please do not get angry; I will speak but once more! Suppose only ten are found there?" And the Lord said, "Then, for the sake of the ten, I will not destroy it."* Persistence in prayer is vital for effective intercession. The more persistent your prayers, the more hope you have that God will answer.

Genesis 32:26-29 *The man said, "Let me go, for it is dawn." But Jacob panted, "I will not let you go unless you bless me." "What is your name?" the man asked. He replied, "Jacob." "Your name will no longer be Jacob," the man told him. "It is now Israel, because you have struggled with both God and men and have won.". . . Then he blessed Jacob there.*

Luke 11:8 *I tell you this—though he won't do it as a friend, if you keep knocking long enough, he will get up and give you what you want so his reputation won't be damaged.*

Persistence is often the key to getting what you want. Just make sure that what you want is in line with God's will for you.

How do I develop persistence?

1 Chronicles 16:11 *Search for the Lord and for his strength, and keep on searching.*

You can develop persistence by continuing steadfastly in prayer and seeking the Lord's desire for your life. The best way to develop persistence is to persist at it.

Proverbs 4:27 *Don't get sidetracked; keep your feet from following evil.*

Avoiding distractions will help you to develop persistence. Distractions lead you away from the goals you have set.

1 Peter 1:13 *So think clearly and exercise self-control. Look forward to the special blessings that will come to you at the return of Jesus Christ.*

Persistence keeps your focus on the task at hand and the promise of blessing to come. To reach your goals, you must persist.

PROMISE FROM GOD: Job 17:9 *The righteous will move onward and forward, and those with pure hearts will become stronger and stronger.*

Poverty

(*see also* FINANCIAL DIFFICULTIES)

Does God really care about the poor?

Psalm 40:17 *I am poor and needy, but the Lord is thinking about me right now.*

Psalm 72:12 *He will rescue the poor when they cry to him; he will help the oppressed, who have no one to defend them.*

Psalm 102:17 *He will listen to the prayers of the destitute. He will not reject their pleas.*
God cares deeply for the poor. He commands all believers to care for them, too. One test of godliness is your care for the poor.

Luke 1:52-53 *He has taken princes from their thrones and exalted the lowly. He has satisfied the hungry with good things and sent the rich away with empty hands.*
God's righteous purposes will one day be fully accomplished. When Jesus returns, all wrongs will be made right. The hungry will be raised up and those whose greed caused their hunger will be cast down.

Does God care that I'm poor? I feel lonely and resentful because so many others have more than they need and I'm struggling.

Hebrews 13:5 *Stay away from the love of money;*

be satisfied with what you have. For God has said,
"I will never fail you. I will never forsake you."

Romans 8:35, 37 *Does it mean he no longer
loves us if we have trouble or calamity, or are persecuted, or are hungry or cold or in danger or threatened with death? . . . No, . . . overwhelming victory
is ours through Christ, who loved us.*
The Bible states again and again that God has a
special concern for the poor. No matter what
your circumstances, God is with you. God is not
in the business of making us rich or poor, but
he is in the business of helping rich or poor walk
with him through life's difficulties.

What is my responsibility to the poor?

Leviticus 25:39 *If any of your Israelite relatives
go bankrupt and sell themselves to you, do not treat
them as slaves.*

Proverbs 19:17 *If you help the poor, you are
lending to the Lord—and he will repay you!*

Proverbs 22:9 *Blessed are those who are generous, because they feed the poor.*

Isaiah 58:10 *Feed the hungry and help those
in trouble. Then your light will shine out from the
darkness, and the darkness around you will be as
bright as day.*
God has compassion for the poor, so if you would
be godly, you must have compassion for the poor.

Compassion that does not reach into your checkbook or onto your "to do" list is philosophical passion, not godly passion. Helping the poor is not merely an obligation; it is a privilege that should bring you great joy. Poverty is not godly, but responding to poverty is.

PROMISE FROM GOD: Proverbs 28:27 *Whoever gives to the poor will lack nothing. But a curse will come upon those who close their eyes to poverty.*

Prayer

What is prayer?

2 Chronicles 7:14 *Then if my people who are called by my name will humble themselves and pray and seek my face and turn from their wicked ways, I will hear from heaven.*

Prayer is an act of humble worship in which we seek God with all our heart. The simplicity of prayer is conversation with the Lord. The majesty of prayer is to humbly enter the very presence of almighty God.

Psalm 38:18 *But I confess my sins; I am deeply sorry for what I have done.*

Prayer often begins with confession of sin. It is through confession that we find forgiveness.

1 Samuel 14:36 *But the priest said, "Let's ask God first."*

2 Samuel 5:19 *So David asked the Lord, "Should I go out to fight the Philistines?"*
Prayer is asking God for guidance and waiting for his direction and leading.

Mark 1:35 *The next morning Jesus awoke long before daybreak and went out alone into the wilderness to pray.*
Prayer is an expression of an intimate relationship with our heavenly Father, who makes his own love and resources available to us.

Psalm 9:1-2 *I will thank you, Lord, with all my heart; . . . I will sing praises to your name, O Most High.*
Through prayer we praise our mighty God.

Does the Bible teach a "right way" to pray?

Psalm 13:1 *O Lord, how long will you forget me? Forever?*
There is no one right way to pray. Honest communication with God and humble listening for God can take many forms. Don't get hung up on whether you're praying correctly. Just pray!

Nehemiah 2:4 *With a prayer to the God of heaven . . .*
The Bible includes examples of silent, spontaneous prayers.

Nehemiah 1:4 *For days I mourned, fasted, and prayed to the God of heaven.*
Effective prayer often includes elements of adoration, confession, and commitment, as well as requests.

Matthew 6:9 *Pray like this: . . .*
Jesus taught his disciples that prayer is an intimate relationship with the Lord that includes a dependence on him for daily needs, a commitment to obedience, and a desire for forgiveness of sin.

Luke 18:1 *One day Jesus told his disciples a story to illustrate their need for constant prayer and to show them that they must never give up.*
It is good to pray consistently and persistently. Persistent prayer is not endless words, but a constant attitude of prayerfulness.

Does God always answer prayer?

Psalm 116:1-2 *I love the Lord because he hears and answers my prayers. Because he bends down and listens, I will pray as long as I have breath!*
God always listens and responds to our prayers. But, as our loving heavenly Father who knows what is best, he does not always give us what we ask for.

2 Corinthians 12:8-9 *Three different times I begged the Lord to take it away. Each time he said, ". . . My power works best in your weakness."*
Sometimes, like Paul, we will find that God

answers prayer by not giving us what we ask for, but something better.

John 14:14 *Yes, ask anything in my name, and I will do it!*
Jesus' name is not a magic wand. Praying in Jesus' name means praying according to Jesus' character and purposes. When we pray like this, we are asking for what God already wants to give us.

Exodus 14:15 *Then the Lord said to Moses, "Why are you crying out to me? Tell the people to get moving!"*
Effective prayer is accompanied by a willingness to obey. When God opens a door, you must walk through it.

PROMISES FROM GOD: **Psalm 9:12** *He does not ignore those who cry to him for help.*

Psalm 145:18 *The Lord is close to all who call on him, yes, to all who call on him sincerely.*

Matthew 7:7 *Keep on asking, and you will be given what you ask for.*

James 5:16 *The earnest prayer of a righteous person has great power and wonderful results.*

1 Peter 3:12 *The eyes of the Lord watch over those who do right, and his ears are open to their prayers.*

Prejudice

What does God think of prejudice?

Galatians 2:12-14 *When he first arrived, he ate with the Gentile Christians, who don't bother with circumcision. But afterward, when some Jewish friends of James came, Peter wouldn't eat with the Gentiles anymore because he was afraid of what these legalists would say. Then the other Jewish Christians followed Peter's hypocrisy, and even Barnabas was influenced to join them in their hypocrisy. When I saw that they were not following the truth of the Good News, I said to Peter in front of all the others, "Since you, a Jew by birth, have discarded the Jewish laws and are living like a Gentile, why are you trying to make these Gentiles obey the Jewish laws you abandoned?"*
Racial prejudice is inconsistent with the Good News of Jesus Christ.

John 1:46 *"Nazareth!" exclaimed Nathanael. "Can anything good come from there?" "Just come and see for yourself," Philip said.*
Jesus broke the stereotypes of his time.

John 4:9 *The woman was surprised, for Jews refuse to have anything to do with Samaritans. She said to Jesus, "You are a Jew, and I am a Samaritan woman. Why are you asking me for a drink?"*
Jesus reached across lines of racial prejudice and division.

Acts 10:28 *Peter told them, "You know it is against the Jewish laws for me to come into a Gentile home like this. But God has shown me that I should never think of anyone as impure."*

God wants us to overcome our racial prejudices. All the things of God are available equally to all people.

What kind of prejudice does God condemn?

1 Samuel 16:7 *Don't judge by his appearance or height. . . . The Lord doesn't make decisions the way you do! People judge by outward appearance, but the Lord looks at a person's thoughts and intentions.*

Isaiah 53:2 *My servant grew up in the Lord's presence like a tender green shoot, sprouting from a root in dry and sterile ground. There was nothing beautiful or majestic about his appearance, nothing to attract us to him.*

God condemns prejudice based on outward appearance. Even Jesus may not have had the tall, handsome body often attributed to him, for Isaiah the prophet said about the coming Savior, "There was nothing beautiful or majestic about his appearance" (Isaiah 53:2).

Esther 3:5-6 *[Haman] was filled with rage. So he decided it was not enough to lay hands on Mordecai alone. . . . He decided to destroy all the Jews throughout the entire empire.*

The Bible encourages us not to form an opinion

about an entire group of people (nationality, church denomination, local club) based on the actions of one individual.

Proverbs 14:20-21 *The poor are despised even by their neighbors, while the rich have many "friends." It is sin to despise one's neighbors; blessed are those who help the poor.*

Proverbs 14:31 *Those who oppress the poor insult their Maker, but those who help the poor honor him.*

James 2:9 *But if you pay special attention to the rich, you are committing a sin.*
God condemns prejudice based on financial well-being or socioeconomic class. Money is not a measure of character.

Matthew 18:10 *Beware that you don't despise a single one of these little ones. For I tell you that in heaven their angels are always in the presence of my heavenly Father.*
How often have you heard the words, "they're just children"? We don't have time for children. We don't listen to them as much as we would to an adult. In fact, children are the true VIPs of the world, for in their hands rests the future.

1 Timothy 4:12 *Don't let anyone think little of you because you are young.*

1 Timothy 5:1 *Never speak harshly to an older man, but appeal to him respectfully as though he were*

your own father. Talk to the younger men as you would to your own brothers.

The Bible forbids discrimination based on age. Maturity is not always a function of age.

Acts 10:28 *Peter told them, "You know it is against the Jewish laws for me to come into a Gentile home like this. But God has shown me that I should never think of anyone as impure."*

Acts 10:34-35 *Then Peter replied, "I see very clearly that God doesn't show partiality. In every nation he accepts those who fear him and do what is right."*

Acts 11:18 *When the others heard this, all their objections were answered and they began praising God. They said, "God has also given the Gentiles the privilege of turning from sin and receiving eternal life."*

God condemns racial prejudice. In heaven there are no ethnic groups, no races, no distinctions such as these, so why should they be important now?

John 1:46 *"Nazareth!" exclaimed Nathanael. "Can anything good come from there?"*

We must not be prejudiced because of the place where a person grew up. The "other side of the tracks" is often viewed negatively, but God lives on both sides of the tracks.

PROMISE FROM GOD: Galatians 3:28 *There is no longer Jew or Gentile, slave or free, male or female. For you are all Christians— you are one in Christ Jesus.*

Presence of God

With all my faults and failures, how can I enter God's presence?

John 14:6 *Jesus told him, "I am the way, the truth, and the life. No one can come to the Father except through me."*

Ephesians 3:12 *Because of Christ and our faith in him, we can now come fearlessly into God's presence, assured of his glad welcome.*

Colossians 1:22 *Yet now he has brought you back as his friends. He has done this through his death on the cross in his own human body. As a result, he has brought you into the very presence of God, and you are holy and blameless as you stand before him without a single fault.*

Hebrews 10:19-22 *And so, dear brothers and sisters, we can boldly enter heaven's Most Holy Place because of the blood of Jesus. This is the new, life-giving way that Christ has opened up for us through the sacred curtain, by means of his death for us. And since we have a great High Priest who rules over*

God's people, let us go right into the presence of God, with true hearts fully trusting him. For our evil consciences have been sprinkled with Christ's blood to make us clean, and our bodies have been washed with pure water.

Because of Jesus Christ's life, death, and resurrection—and your faith in him—you stand holy and blameless in the presence of God.

What can keep me from enjoying God's presence?

Isaiah 59:2 *But there is a problem—your sins have cut you off from God. Because of your sin, he has turned away and will not listen anymore.*

Colossians 1:21 *This includes you who were once so far away from God. You were his enemies, separated from him by your evil thoughts and actions.*

1 Corinthians 6:9 *Don't you know that those who do wrong will have no share in the Kingdom of God?*

Galatians 5:19-21 *When you follow the desires of your sinful nature, your lives will produce these evil results: sexual immorality, impure thoughts, eagerness for lustful pleasure, idolatry, participation in demonic activities, hostility, quarreling, jealousy, outbursts of anger, selfish ambition, divisions, the feeling that everyone is wrong except those in your own little group, envy, drunkenness, wild parties, and* other kinds of sin. Let me tell you again, as I have before, that anyone living that sort of life will not inherit the Kingdom of God.

1 Peter 3:12 *The eyes of the Lord watch over those who do right, and his ears are open to their prayers. But the Lord turns his face against those who do evil.*

Revelation 21:27 *Nothing evil will be allowed to enter—no one who practices shameful idolatry and dishonesty—but only those whose names are written in the Lamb's Book of Life.*

Sin keeps you from fully enjoying God's presence because sin separates you from your holy God. Though forgiveness of sin restores you to enter into God's presence as a daily relationship, you will one day experience the complete wonder and intimacy of his presence in eternity.

How can I experience God's presence for today on earth and for eternity in heaven?

James 4:8 *Draw close to God, and God will draw close to you. Wash your hands, you sinners; purify your hearts, you hypocrites.*

Deuteronomy 4:29 *From there you will search again for the Lord your God. And if you search for him with all your heart and soul, you will find him.* God is with you everywhere and you can draw near to him at any time.

Hebrews 11:6 *So, you see, it is impossible to please God without faith. Anyone who wants to come to him must believe that there is a God and that he rewards those who sincerely seek him.*

Revelation 3:20 *Look! Here I stand at the door and knock. If you hear me calling and open the door, I will come in, and we will share a meal as friends.* You must believe that he is, before you can believe that he is with you.

Matthew 18:3 *Then he said, "I assure you, unless you turn from your sins and become as little children, you will never get into the Kingdom of Heaven."*

Matthew 5:20 *But I warn you—unless you obey God better than the teachers of religious law and the Pharisees do, you can't enter the Kingdom of Heaven at all!*

There is only one way to experience God's eternal presence—turn from your sins, ask God to forgive your sins, and ask Jesus to be Lord of your life.

John 14:23 *Jesus replied, "All those who love me will do what I say. My Father will love them, and we will come to them and live with them."*

Psalm 16:11 *You will show me the way of life, granting me the joy of your presence and the pleasures of living with you forever.*

God longs for you to enjoy fellowship with him. God's solution to the sin in your life is for you to come to him through believing and accepting

Jesus' payment for your sin, turning from your sin, and obeying God. You experience God's presence daily as you look to him and for him.

What are some of the benefits of being in God's presence?

Philippians 2:13 *For God is working in you, giving you the desire to obey him and the power to do what pleases him.*
God's presence helps us to obey and please him.

2 Corinthians 3:17 *Now, the Lord is the Spirit, and wherever the Spirit of the Lord is, he gives freedom.*
In God's presence, we have freedom from our slavery to sin.

Romans 8:9-10 *But you are not controlled by your sinful nature. You are controlled by the Spirit ifyou have the Spirit of God living in you. (And remember that those who do not have the Spirit of Christ living in them are not Christians at all.) Since Christ lives within you, even though your body will die because of sin, your spirit is alive because you have been made right with God.*
We have eternal life because of his presence.

Isaiah 43:2 *When you go through deep waters and great trouble, I will be with you. When you go through rivers of difficulty, you will not drown! When you walk through the fire of oppression, you will not be burned up; the flames will not consume you.*

Psalm 23:4 *Even when I walk through the dark valley of death, I will not be afraid, for you are close beside me. Your rod and your staff protect and comfort me.*

His presence gives us protection and comfort.

Deuteronomy 20:1 *When you go out to fight your enemies and you face horses and chariots and an army greater than your own, do not be afraid. The Lord your God, who brought you safely out of Egypt, is with you!*

Joshua 1:9 *I command you—be strong and courageous! Do not be afraid or discouraged. For the Lord your God is with you wherever you go.*

God's presence gives us courage.

Psalm 63:8 *I follow close behind you; your strong right hand holds me securely.*

Psalm 40:1-2 *I waited patiently for the Lord to help me, and he turned to me and heard my cry. He lifted me out of the pit of despair, out of the mud and the mire. He set my feet on solid ground and steadied me as I walked along.*

We have security because of his presence.

Acts 2:28 *You have shown me the way of life, and you will give me wonderful joy in your presence.*

Psalm 16:8-9, 11 *I know the Lord is always with me. I will not be shaken, for he is right beside me. No wonder my heart is filled with joy, and my*

*mouth shouts his praises! My body rests in safety. . . .
You will show me the way of life, granting me the
joy of your presence and the pleasures of living with
you forever.*

We experience joy in his presence.

How does God's presence in my life affect my relationships?

Galatians 5:22-23 *But when the Holy Spirit
controls our lives, he will produce this kind of fruit
in us: love, joy, peace, patience, kindness, goodness,
faithfulness, gentleness, and self-control. Here there
is no conflict with the law.*

God's presence in your life fully equips you for
healthy relationships with one another.

Psalm 34:18 *The Lord is close to the brokenhearted; he rescues those who are crushed in spirit.*

When your earthly relationships injure you,
God is able to provide comfort, healing, and
restoration.

How can I be assured of God's presence?

Psalm 23:6 *Surely your goodness and unfailing
love will pursue me all the days of my life, and I will
live in the house of the Lord forever.*

Psalm 139:5, 7 *You both precede and follow
me. You place your hand of blessing on my head. . . .
I can never escape from your spirit! I can never get
away from your presence!*

Romans 8:38-39 *And I am convinced that nothing can ever separate us from his love. Death can't, and life can't. The angels can't, and the demons can't. Our fears for today, our worries about tomorrow, and even the powers of hell can't keep God's love away. Whether we are high above the sky or in the deepest ocean, nothing in all creation will ever be able to separate us from the love of God that is revealed in Christ Jesus our Lord.*

His presence is always with you. Nothing can separate you from his love for you. The Word of God assures you of this.

Psalm 16:8 *I know the Lord is always with me. I will not be shaken, for he is right beside me.*

Psalm 121:3-4 *He will not let you stumble and fall; the one who watches over you will not sleep. Indeed, he who watches over Israel never tires and never sleeps.*

Psalm 34:18-19 *The Lord is close to the broken-hearted; he rescues those who are crushed in spirit. The righteous face many troubles, but the Lord rescues them from each and every one.*

Matthew 28:20 *Teach these new disciples to obey all the commands I have given you. And be sure of this: I am with you always, even to the end of the age.*

God's presence is with you regardless of life's circumstances. The Word of God assures you of this.

What should I do when it feels like God is far away?

Psalm 139:7 *I can never escape from your spirit! I can never get away from your presence!*
God will go to any height or depth to be with you.

Job 23:8 *I go east. . . . I go west, but I cannot find him.*
Faith is trusting, even when you feel far from God. When you cannot find him, wait. He will find you.

PROMISES FROM GOD: Leviticus 26:12 *I will walk among you; I will be your God.*

Joshua 1:9 *The Lord your God is with you wherever you go.*

Psalm 16:8, 11 *I know the Lord is always with me. I will not be shaken, for he is right beside me. . . . You will show me the way of life, granting me the joy of your presence and the pleasures of living with you forever.*

Psalm 145:18 *The Lord is close to all who call on him.*

Isaiah 43:2 *When you go through deep waters and great trouble, I will be with you.*

Isaiah 46:4 *I will be your God throughout your lifetime—until your hair is white with age. I made you, and I will care for you. I will carry you along and save you.*

Pressure

(see also STRESS)

What are some of the dangers of pressure?

Luke 10:40-41 *But Martha was worrying over the big dinner she was preparing. She came to Jesus and said, "Lord, doesn't it seem unfair to you that my sister just sits here while I do all the work? Tell her to come and help me." But the Lord said to her, "My dear Martha, you are so upset over all these details!"*

Matthew 13:22 *The thorny ground represents those who hear and accept the Good News, but all too quickly the message is crowded out by the cares of this life and the lure of wealth, so no crop is produced.*

Pressure can cause us to focus on the unimportant and miss the important. As pressure squeezes our perspective inward, we lose our perspective outward. Preoccupation with the trivia of the moment blinds us to the big picture.

Mark 14:38 *Keep alert and pray. Otherwise temptation will overpower you. For though the spirit is willing enough, the body is weak.*

Pressure often makes us vulnerable to temptation, for it weakens our resistance.

1 Kings 11:4 *In Solomon's old age, they turned his heart to worship their gods instead of trusting only in the Lord his God, as his father, David, had done.*

Pressure can make us rationalize sin and compromise our beliefs. The pressure of the seduction of riches may so occupy our hearts that we leave no room for God. Lust crowds out true love, whether in our relationship with our spouse or with God.

P s a l m   6 : 7 *My vision is blurred by grief; my eyes are worn out because of all my enemies.*

P s a l m   7 7 : 2 - 3 *When I was in deep trouble, I searched for the Lord. All night long I pray, with hands lifted toward heaven, pleading. There can be no joy for me until he acts. I think of God, and I moan, overwhelmed with longing for his help.* Pressure can have negative physical effects. The mind, soul, and body are interrelated. As one malfunctions, the others may get out of sync. Spiritual distress can induce physical or mental distress, just as physical or mental distress can induce sickness in our soul.

Is pressure ever positive?

J a m e s   1 : 2 - 4 *Dear brothers and sisters, whenever trouble comes your way, let it be an opportunity for joy. For when your faith is tested, your endurance has a chance to grow. So let it grow, for when your endurance is fully developed, you will be strong in character and ready for anything.*

R o m a n s   5 : 3 *We can rejoice, too, when we run into problems and trials, for we know that they are good for us—they help us learn to endure.*

2 Chronicles 32:31 *However, when ambassadors arrived from Babylon to ask about the remarkable events that had taken place in the land, God withdrew from Hezekiah in order to test him and to see what was really in his heart.*

Pressure can test and develop strength of character. The question is not whether we will have pressure, but what will we do with pressure when it comes. If we deal with pressure with our own strength, we may be quickly and easily overcome. If we let God help us deal with our pressure, we can come out stronger and more joyful.

Hebrews 3:7, 13, 15 *That is why the Holy Spirit says, "Today you must listen to his voice.". . . You must warn each other every day, as long as it is called "today," so that none of you will be deceived by sin and hardened against God. . . . But never forget the warning: "Today you must listen to his voice. Don't harden your hearts against him as Israel did when they rebelled."*

The urgency of God's pressure can be positive. God presses us to a decision while the time is right. To respond to his pressure has everlasting benefits. To ignore it will lead to everlasting disaster.

1 Peter 1:17 *And remember that the heavenly Father to whom you pray has no favorites when he judges. He will judge or reward you according*

to what you do. So you must live in reverent fear of him during your time as foreigners here on earth.
The pressure of the coming judgment day can encourage us to right living today. A casual attitude toward the coming judgment can encourage us to wrong living today.

Ecclesiastes 12:11 *A wise teacher's words spur students to action and emphasize important truths. The collected sayings of the wise are like guidance from a shepherd.*
The pressure to learn is positive, especially learning the Scriptures, for learning God's ways brings wisdom and life.

How can I best handle pressure?

Mark 14:35-36 *He went on a little farther and fell face down on the ground. He prayed that, if it were possible, the awful hour awaiting him might pass him by. "Abba, Father," he said, "everything is possible for you. Please take this cup of suffering away from me. Yet I want your will, not mine."*
You should follow Jesus' example of praying to God, seeking support from other Christians, and focusing on God's will.

Matthew 4:10 *"Get out of here, Satan," Jesus told him. "For the Scriptures say, 'You must worship the Lord your God; serve only him.'"*

Psalm 119:143 *As pressure and stress bear down on me, I find joy in your commands.*

233

You should immerse yourself in and obey God's Word. The more you find joy in the Lord, the less you will feel stress from external pressures.

Exodus 18:17-18, 24 *"This is not good!" his father-in-law exclaimed. "You're going to wear yourself out—and the people, too. This job is too heavy a burden for you to handle all by yourself."... Moses listened to his father-in-law's advice and followed his suggestions.*

You should listen to godly counsel. Delegation is often an overlooked solution to the mounting pressure you feel from trying to do everything yourself.

Daniel 3:14, 16-18 *Nebuchadnezzar said to them, "Is it true, Shadrach, Meshach, and Abednego, that you refuse to serve my gods or to worship the gold statue I have set up?"... Shadrach, Meshach, and Abednego replied, "O Nebuchadnezzar, we do not need to defend ourselves before you. If we are thrown into the blazing furnace, the God whom we serve is able to save us. He will rescue us from your power, Your Majesty. But even if he doesn't, Your Majesty can be sure that we will never serve your gods or worship the gold statue you have set up."*

Genesis 39:10, 12 *She kept putting pressure on him day after day, but he refused to sleep with her, and he kept out of her way as much as possible....*

*She came and grabbed him by his shirt, demanding,
"Sleep with me!" Joseph tore himself away . . . [and]
ran from the house.*

The pressure you feel from temptation to sin can
best be handled by acknowledging sin as sin and
standing firm in your commitment to God. Standing firm sometimes means physically fleeing from
things that bring oppressive pressures.

Matthew 11:28-30 *Then Jesus said, "Come
to me, all of you who are weary and carry heavy
burdens, and I will give you rest. Take my yoke upon
you. Let me teach you, because I am humble and
gentle, and you will find rest for your souls. For my
yoke fits perfectly, and the burden I give you is light."*

1 Peter 5:7 *Give all your worries and cares to
God, for he cares about what happens to you.*
You should prayerfully enjoy the peace of know-
ing that God is in control.

How can I resist negative peer pressure?

James 4:17 *Remember, it is sin to know what
you ought to do and then not do it.*

1 Corinthians 10:13 *But remember that the
temptations that come into your life are no different
from what others experience. And God is faithful. He
will keep the temptation from becoming so strong that
you can't stand up against it. When you are tempted,
he will show you a way out so that you will not give
in to it.*

You must look for God's way out in every tempting situation. God's way may take you away from, around, above, or through the temptation, but it will get you safely to the other side.

Exodus 23:2 *Do not join a crowd that intends to do evil. When you are on the witness stand, do not be swayed in your testimony by the opinion of the majority.*

Proverbs 24:1 *Don't envy evil people; don't desire their company.*
The best way to resist negative peer pressure is to choose wise peers.

Matthew 1:20, 24 *As he considered this, he fell asleep, and an angel of the Lord appeared to him in a dream. "Joseph, son of David," the angel said, "do not be afraid to go ahead with your marriage to Mary. For the child within her has been conceived by the Holy Spirit."... When Joseph woke up, he did what the angel of the Lord commanded. He brought Mary home to be his wife.*
You must obey God no matter what others may think. What God thinks of you is infinitely more important than what others think of you.

Matthew 14:9 *The king was sorry, but because of his oath and because he didn't want to back down in front of his guests, he issued the necessary orders.*
You must never let your pride or the risk of embarrassment keep you from making right choices.

How can I help others who are under pressure?

Philippians 2:4 *Don't think only about your own affairs, but be interested in others, too, and what they are doing.*

You can avoid becoming so preoccupied with your own pressures that you become insensitive to the pressure others face. Often as you help others with their pressures, you may relieve your own.

1 Corinthians 8:9 *But you must be careful with this freedom of yours. Do not cause a brother or sister with a weaker conscience to stumble.*

Don't allow your lifestyle to create additional pressures for others. A strong Christian may handle a lifestyle that would be a disastrous model for a weaker Christian.

Hebrews 10:24 *Think of ways to encourage one another to outbursts of love and good deeds.*

Proverbs 27:17 *As iron sharpens iron, a friend sharpens a friend.*

Proverbs 12:25 *Worry weighs a person down; an encouraging word cheers a person up.*

Be an encouragement to others who are under pressure.

Are there ways I can prevent—or minimize—pressure?

1 Kings 22:13-14 *Meanwhile, the messenger who went to get Micaiah said to him, "Look, all the*

237

prophets are promising victory for the king. Be sure that you agree with them and promise success." But Micaiah replied, "As surely as the Lord lives, I will say only what the Lord tells me to say."

You can determine to be faithful to God *before* the time of pressure comes. Then you don't have to make that decision when you're under pressure.

Psalm 38:4 *My guilt overwhelms me—it is a burden too heavy to bear.*

You can obey God, for meeting pressure his way will bring you peace.

1 Corinthians 15:33 *Don't be fooled by those who say such things, for "bad company corrupts good character."*

Psalm 1:1 *Oh, the joys of those who do not follow the advice of the wicked, or stand around with sinners, or join in with scoffers.*

You can respond to ungodly pressures better when you choose godly companions and counselors.

PROMISE FROM GOD: Psalm 55:22 *Give your burdens to the Lord, and he will take care of you. He will not permit the godly to slip and fall.*

Problems

(*see also* ADVERSITY)

How does God view my problems?

1 Peter 5:7 *Give all your worries and cares to God, for he cares about what happens to you.*
God cares about you and your problems.

Psalm 145:14 *The Lord helps the fallen and lifts up those bent beneath their loads.*
God is not only aware of your problems but wants to help you resolve them.

Acts 8:4 *But the believers who had fled Jerusalem went everywhere preaching the Good News about Jesus.*
God may use your problems to give you unexpected assignments.

How can I anticipate problems and prepare for them?

Colossians 2:6-7 *And now, just as you accepted Christ Jesus as your Lord, you must continue to live in obedience to him. Let your roots grow down into him and draw up nourishment from him, so you will grow in faith, strong and vigorous in the truth.*

Jude 20-21 *But you, dear friends, must continue to build your lives on the foundation of your holy faith. And continue to pray as you are directed by the Holy Spirit. Live in such a way that God's love can*

bless you as you wait for the eternal life that our Lord Jesus Christ in his mercy is going to give you.
Realize that problems are inevitable; they will come. So the question is not, "Will problems come?" but "What will I do with problems when they come?"

Ephesians 6:11-12 *Put on all of God's armor so that you will be able to stand firm against all strategies and tricks of the Devil. For we are not fighting against people made of flesh and blood, but against the evil rulers and authorities of the unseen world, against those mighty powers of darkness who rule this world, and against wicked spirits in the heavenly realms.*
You can best prepare for life's inevitable problems by living a life of faith, love, obedience, and prayer. You are encouraged to be strong with God's power. If you go onto life's battlefields already equipped with God's spiritual armor, you will more quickly and easily win the battles that your problems bring. The heat of battle is no time to be looking for armor and reading a manual about the way to use it.

How can I best cope with life's problems?

Philippians 4:6 *Don't worry about anything; instead, pray about everything. Tell God what you need, and thank him for all he has done.*

Psalm 56:3-4 *But when I am afraid, I put my trust in you. O God, I praise your word. I trust in*

240

God, so why should I be afraid? What can mere mortals do to me?

Isaiah 26:3 *You will keep in perfect peace all who trust in you, whose thoughts are fixed on you!* God is your first and primary point of confidence and trust as you communicate with him honestly about your worries and fears. At times your problems are just too big for you. So you need someone bigger, wiser, and stronger than you or your problems to help, and that is God.

Psalm 119:24 *Your decrees please me; they give me wise advice.*

Galatians 6:2 *Share each other's troubles and problems, and in this way obey the law of Christ.*

Exodus 18:17-18 *"This is not good!" his father-in-law exclaimed. "You're going to wear yourself out—and the people, too. This job is too heavy a burden for you to handle all by yourself."* Godly people can be a source of godly counsel.

Acts 16:22-25 *A mob quickly formed against Paul and Silas, and the city officials ordered them stripped and beaten with wooden rods. They were severely beaten, and then they were thrown into prison. The jailer was ordered to make sure they didn't escape. So he took no chances but put them into the inner dungeon and clamped their feet in the stocks. Around midnight, Paul and Silas were praying and singing hymns to God, and the other prisoners were listening.*

James 1:2 *Dear brothers and sisters, whenever trouble comes your way, let it be an opportunity for joy.* Your problems do not have to weaken your faith, praise, or joy. Seeking God's solutions for your problems can enhance your faith, praise, and joy.

How should I learn and grow from my problems?

Psalm 107:43 *Those who are wise will take all this to heart; they will see in our history the faithful love of the Lord.*
The more you see God at work in your problems, the more you learn about his faithful, loving character in your life. The more you learn about what God does, the more you will want to learn about who he is.

James 1:2-4, 12 *Dear brothers and sisters, whenever trouble comes your way, let it be an opportunity for joy. For when your faith is tested, your endurance has a chance to grow. So let it grow, for when your endurance is fully developed, you will be strong in character and ready for anything. . . . God blesses the people who patiently endure testing.*
The more you endure life's problems, the more you see your own character strengthened. The more you become the kind of person God desires, the more you can do the kind of work God desires.

Philippians 4:12-13 *I have learned the secret of living in every situation, whether it is with a full stomach or empty, with plenty or little. For I can do everything with the help of Christ who gives me the strength I need.*

2 Corinthians 1:8-9 *We were crushed and completely overwhelmed, and we thought we would never live through it. In fact, we expected to die. But as a result, we learned not to rely on ourselves, but on God who can raise the dead.*

The more you endure life's problems, the more you learn the source of your strength and your help. When you realize the source of your strength, you should have the good sense to go to that source of strength.

How can I help others in the midst of their problems?

Hebrews 13:1-2 *Continue to love each other with true Christian love. Don't forget to show hospitality to strangers, for some who have done this have entertained angels without realizing it!*

Philippians 4:14 *But even so, you have done well to share with me in my present difficulty.*

Obadiah 12 *You shouldn't have done this! You shouldn't have gloated when they exiled your relatives to distant lands. You shouldn't have rejoiced because they were suffering such misfortune. You shouldn't have crowed over them as they suffered these disasters.*

2 Corinthians 1:3-4 *All praise to the God and Father of our Lord Jesus Christ. He is the source of every mercy and the God who comforts us. He comforts us in all our troubles so that we can comfort others. When others are troubled, we will be able to give them the same comfort God has given us.*
You can genuinely love others with your actions, your emotions, your attitudes, your words, and your presence. Love resolves a thousand problems and prevents a thousand more.

PROMISE FROM GOD: Philippians 4:6 *Don't worry about anything; instead, pray about everything. Tell God what you need, and thank him for all he has done.*

Promises

Are God's promises really trustworthy?

Joshua 23:14 *Deep in your hearts you know that every promise of the Lord your God has come true. Not a single one has failed!*

Numbers 23:19 *God is not a man, that he should lie. He is not human, that he should change his mind. Has he ever spoken and failed to act? Has he ever promised and not carried it through?* God's promises are completely trustworthy! A promise from God is a down payment on the character of God. The promises from a perfect God cannot fail.

Why does it sometimes seem as if God hasn't fulfilled his promises?

2 Peter 3:8 *But you must not forget, dear friends, that a day is like a thousand years to the Lord, and a thousand years is like a day.*

Habakkuk 2:3 *Surely these things I plan won't happen right away. Slowly, steadily, surely, the time approaches when the vision will be fulfilled. If it seems slow, wait patiently, for it will surely take place. It will not be delayed.*

God will fulfill his promises, but sometimes his timetable is different from ours. We are called to wait and trust, confident in God's truthfulness.

With so little to depend on in life, what can I count on from God?

Ephesians 1:14 *The Spirit is God's guarantee that he will give us everything he promised.*

The Holy Spirit is God's guarantee that his promises are trustworthy.

John 14:2 *I am going to prepare a place for you. If this were not so, I would tell you plainly.*

Jesus promises an eternal home in heaven for those who trust him.

John 14:16-17 *And I will ask the Father, and he will give you another Counselor, who will never leave*

you. He is the Holy Spirit.
Jesus promises to be with you forever in the form of the Holy Spirit.

Hebrews 6:18 *God has given us both his promise and his oath. These two things are unchangeable.*
God's promises are completely dependable and trustworthy because God himself is so. This can give you great comfort in the present and assurance for the future. If the past and present verify God's dependability, the future will certainly anticipate his continued dependability.

PROMISE FROM GOD: Hebrews 10:23 *God can be trusted to keep his promise.*

Protection

Does God promise to protect me?

Psalm 31:19 *You have done so much for those who come to you for protection.*

Daniel 3:17-18 *The God whom we serve is able to save us, . . . but even if he doesn't . . .*
God promises to protect and keep safe those who love him. But the ultimate fulfillment of this promise is in the spiritual protection of God's loving grace rather than physical protection. Christians will be saved from eternal destruction. Like Daniel's friends, you must commit yourself

to obeying God no matter what happens to your earthly body.

Psalm 17:8, 15 *Guard me as the apple of your eye. . . . When I awake, I will be fully satisfied, for I will see you face to face.*
The psalmist prayed to God for protection from enemies, yet trusted that ultimate safety is God's salvation that leads to the hope of heaven.

Philippians 4:7 *His peace will guard your hearts and minds as you live in Christ Jesus.*
Through consistent and devoted prayer you can know the protection of God's supernatural peace.

PROMISES FROM GOD: Joshua 23:10 *For the Lord your God fights for you, just as he has promised.*

Psalm 121:8 *The Lord keeps watch over you as you come and go, both now and forever.*

Purpose

How do I find true purpose in life?
Psalm 40:8 *I take joy in doing your will, my God, for your law is written on my heart.*

Ecclesiastes 12:13 *Here is my final conclusion: Fear God and obey his commands, for this is the duty of every person.*
Meaning in life comes from obeying God and

doing his will—both his will for all believers, which is found in the Bible and his will for you, which is discovered through prayer and deepening your relationship with him. The ultimate goal in life is not to reach destinations where you want to go but to reach destinations where God wants you to go.

John 17:4 *I brought glory to you here on earth by doing everything you told me to do.*

Romans 11:36 *Everything comes from him; everything exists by his power and is intended for his glory.*
Your purpose in life is to honor, obey, and praise the Lord. All meaningful human effort comes by doing these things and therefore brings glory to God.

Matthew 28:18-20 *Jesus came and told his disciples, "I have been given complete authority in heaven and on earth. Therefore, go and make disciples of all the nations, baptizing them in the name of the Father and the Son and the Holy Spirit. Teach these new disciples to obey all the commands I have given you. And be sure of this: I am with you always, even to the end of the age."*
Part of your purpose in life includes taking part in fulfilling the great commission to tell others about Jesus and in building the Kingdom of God.

Does God have a special purpose for me?

Acts 20:24 *My life is worth nothing unless I use it for doing the work assigned me by the Lord Jesus— the work of telling others the Good News about God's wonderful kindness and love.*

God has given you work to do, which is part of his purpose to bring his Good News of salvation to all creatures. Divine directives are significant purposes.

2 Timothy 1:9 *It is God who saved us and chose us to live a holy life. He did this not because we deserved it, but because that was his plan long before the world began—to show his love and kindness to us through Christ Jesus.*

How wonderful to think that God wants to show his love and kindness to you so that you can grow in your relationship with him and see how to live a holy life.

How can I know God's purpose for my life?

Philippians 1:20 *For I live in eager expectation and hope . . . that I will always be bold for Christ . . . and that my life will always honor Christ.*

Philippians 3:12 *I keep working toward that day when I will finally be all that Christ Jesus saved me for and wants me to be.*

Paul's great purpose, whether by life or death, was to win others to Christ.

Acts 13:2 *One day as these men were worshiping the Lord and fasting, the Holy Spirit said, "Dedicate Barnabas and Saul for the special work I have for them."* Worship, prayer, fasting, and relationships with other believers will help you to discern God's plan for your life.

PROMISE FROM GOD: Romans 12:2 *Let God transform you into a new person by changing the way you think. Then you will know what God wants you to do, and you will know how good and pleasing and perfect his will really is.*

Quitting

(*see also* ENDURANCE or PERSEVERANCE)

How can I keep going when I feel like quitting?

2 Corinthians 4:8 *We are pressed on every side by troubles, but we are not crushed and broken. We are perplexed, but we don't give up and quit.* Even in the midst of suffering, believers can find strength to endure for Christ.

2 Timothy 4:7 *I have fought a good fight, I have finished the race, and I have remained faithful.*

Galatians 6:9 *Don't get tired of doing what is good. Don't get discouraged and give up, for we will reap a harvest of blessing at the appropriate time.*

You can avoid discouragement and the desire to quit by keeping your eyes on the goal and reward of heaven.

PROMISE FROM GOD: Matthew 10:22 *And everyone will hate you because of your allegiance to me. But those who endure to the end will be saved.*

Refreshment

Why do I need refreshment?

Psalm 73:26 *My health may fail, and my spirit may grow weak, but God remains the strength of my heart; he is mine forever.*

Isaiah 40:30-31 *Even youths will become exhausted, and young men will give up. But those who wait on the Lord will find new strength.*

2 Corinthians 5:2 *We grow weary in our present bodies, and we long for the day when we will put on our heavenly bodies like new clothing.*

Galatians 6:9 *So don't get tired of doing what is good. Don't get discouraged and give up, for we will reap a harvest of blessing at the appropriate time.*

Whether it be from physical or emotional exhaustion, you need refreshment to renew your soul, your mind, and your body.

How can my soul be refreshed?

Psalm 63:1 *O God, you are my God; I earnestly search for you. My soul thirsts for you; my whole body longs for you in this parched and weary land where there is no water.*

Psalm 90:14 *Satisfy us in the morning with your unfailing love, so we may sing for joy to the end of our lives.*
Through God's faithful, loving character.

Matthew 11:28 *Then Jesus said, "Come to me, all of you who are weary and carry heavy burdens, and I will give you rest."*
Through your relationship with Jesus.

Psalm 19:7 *The law of the Lord is perfect, reviving the soul. The decrees of the Lord are trustworthy, making wise the simple.*

Psalm 119:50 *Your promise revives me; it comforts me in all my troubles.*
Through God's Word.

Mark 1:35 *The next morning Jesus awoke long before daybreak and went out alone into the wilderness to pray.*
Through time spent alone with God in prayer.

Ezekiel 18:31 *Put all your rebellion behind you, and get for yourselves a new heart and a new spirit. For why should you die, O people of Israel?*

Ezekiel 36:26 *And I will give you a new heart with new and right desires, and I will put a new spirit in you. I will take out your stony heart of sin and give you a new, obedient heart.*

Through obedience.

Acts 3:19-20 *Now turn from your sins and turn to God, so you can be cleansed of your sins. Then wonderful times of refreshment will come from the presence of the Lord, and he will send Jesus your Messiah to you again.*

Through confession and repentance of sin.

Hebrews 12:11-12 *No discipline is enjoyable while it is happening—it is painful! But afterward there will be a quiet harvest of right living for those who are trained in this way. So take a new grip with your tired hands and stand firm on your shaky legs.*

Through accepting God's discipline, which brings the joy of a restored relationship with him.

2 Corinthians 4:16-17 *That is why we never give up. Though our bodies are dying, our spirits are being renewed every day. For our present troubles are quite small and won't last very long. Yet they produce for us an immeasurably great glory that will last forever!*

Through maintaining an eternal perspective.

Proverbs 11:25 *The generous prosper and are satisfied; those who refresh others will themselves be refreshed.*

Through ministering to others.

How can my mind be refreshed?

Psalm 94:19 *When doubts filled my mind, your comfort gave me renewed hope and cheer.*
Through God's comfort. Doubts can clutter your mind. God's comfort sweeps the clutter away and refreshes your mind.

2 Peter 3:1-2 *This is my second letter to you, dear friends, and in both of them I have tried to stimulate your wholesome thinking and refresh your memory. I want you to remember and understand what the holy prophets said long ago and what our Lord and Savior commanded through your apostles.*
Through God's Word. Your mind is refreshed most by knowing the mind of God through his Word.

Colossians 3:10 *In its place you have clothed yourselves with a brand-new nature that is continually being renewed as you learn more and more about Christ, who created this new nature within you.*
Through learning about Jesus. When Jesus creates a new nature in you, he creates a new mind and a new attitude, and that is refreshing.

Romans 12:2 *Don't copy the behavior and customs of this world, but let God transform you into a new person by changing the way you think.*

Romans 8:5 *Those who are dominated by the sinful nature think about sinful things, but those who*

are controlled by the Holy Spirit think about things
that please the Spirit.
Through thinking on things pleasing to the Holy
Spirit. A mind in harmony with the Holy Spirit
will be refreshed.

How can my body be refreshed?

Psalm 92:10 *But you have made me as strong
as a wild bull. How refreshed I am by your power!*
Through God's power.

Psalm 145:16 *When you open your hand, you
satisfy the hunger and thirst of every living thing.*
Through God's provision.

Exodus 23:12 *Work for six days, and rest on the
seventh. . . . It will also allow the people of your household, including your slaves and visitors, to be refreshed.*
Through rest.

Exodus 17:12 *Moses' arms finally became too
tired to hold up the staff any longer. So Aaron and
Hur found a stone for him to sit on. Then they stood
on each side, holding up his hands until sunset.*
Through physical assistance from others.

Proverbs 3:7-8 *Don't be impressed with your
own wisdom. Instead, fear the Lord and turn your
back on evil. Then you will gain renewed health and
vitality.*
Through right living.

How can I refresh others?

2 Timothy 1:16 *May the Lord show special kindness to Onesiphorus and all his family because he often visited and encouraged me. He was never ashamed of me because I was in prison.*

Philemon 7 *I myself have gained much joy and comfort from your love, my brother, because your kindness has so often refreshed the hearts of God's people.*

With your acts of kindness.

Proverbs 25:25 *Good news from far away is like cold water to the thirsty.*

Proverbs 18:4 *A person's words can be life-giving water; words of true wisdom are as refreshing as a bubbling brook.*

Proverbs 18:20 *Words satisfy the soul as food satisfies the stomach; the right words on a person's lips bring satisfaction.*

Isaiah 50:4 *The Sovereign Lord has given me his words of wisdom, so that I know what to say to all these weary ones. Morning by morning he wakens me and opens my understanding to his will.*

With your words.

PROMISE FROM GOD: Psalm 73:26 *My health may fail, and my spirit may grow weak, but God remains the strength of my heart; he is mine forever.*

Regrets

How can I deal with the regrets of my life?

2 Corinthians 5:17 *What this means is that those who become Christians become new persons. They are not the same anymore, for the old life is gone. A new life has begun!*

Trust in Christ to forgive your past and give you a fresh start from God. What you regret cannot be retracted, but it can be forgiven and forgotten.

Psalm 51:1, 12 *Blot out the stain of my sins. . . . Restore to me again the joy of your salvation.*

Micah 7:19 *Once again you will have compassion on us. You will trample our sins under your feet and throw them into the depths of the ocean!*

You deal with regrets caused by sin by confessing the sin and receiving God's forgiveness. Because God no longer holds your sins against you, you no longer have to hold them against yourself. A slate wiped clean of regrets is the best way to deal with regrets.

How can I avoid regrets in the future?

1 Thessalonians 5:22 *Keep away from every kind of evil.*

Commit yourself decisively to a life of godliness and obedience.

Psalm 1:1-2 *Oh, the joys of those who do not follow the advice of the wicked, or stand around with sinners, or join in with scoffers. But they delight in doing everything the Lord wants; day and night they think about his law.*
Immerse yourself in Scripture and surround yourself with positive influences.

PROMISE FROM GOD: 2 Corinthians 7:10 *For God can use sorrow in our lives to help us turn away from sin and seek salvation. We will never regret that kind of sorrow.*

Rejection

(*see also* ABANDONMENT)

How can I recover from rejection in my life?

1 Peter 5:7 *Give all your worries and cares to God, for he cares about what happens to you.*
Don't try to deal with rejection by yourself. Bring your concerns to God.

Romans 8:38 *I am convinced that nothing can ever separate us from his love.*
Remember that, though others may reject you, nothing can separate you from God's love!

Will God ever reject me?

John 8:10-11 *"Didn't even one of them*

condemn you?" "No, Lord," she said. And Jesus said, "Neither do I. Go and sin no more."
God rejects the sin without rejecting the sinner.

John 6:37 *Those the Father has given me will come to me, and I will never reject them.*
The Lord accepts all who come to him in faith.

PROMISE FROM GOD: Psalm 94:14 *The Lord will not reject his people.*

Repentance

(*see also* FORGIVENESS or SALVATION)

What is repentance?

Matthew 3:2 *Turn from your sins and turn to God.*
Repentance means being sorry for sin and being committed to a new way of life—that of serving God. When God forgives our sins, we have a new sense of hope for the future.

Luke. 19:8 *Zacchaeus . . . said to the Lord, ". . . If I have overcharged people on their taxes, I will give them back four times as much!"*
Repentance is made complete by changed behavior, giving us hope that our lives will be truly different.

Exodus 9:34 *When Pharaoh saw this, he and his officials sinned yet again by stubbornly refusing to do as they had promised.*

Repentance that produces no lasting change is insincere and dashes our hopes. Repentance is not merely intending to turn from sin, but doing it.

Why does God want us to repent?

2 Chronicles 30:9 *For the Lord your God is gracious and merciful. If you return to him, he will not continue to turn his face from you.*
Repentance is necessary if we are to hope for an ongoing relationship with God.

1 Samuel 7:3 *Samuel said to all the people of Israel, "If you are really serious about wanting to return to the Lord, get rid of your foreign gods. . . . Determine to obey only the Lord; then he will rescue you."*
We need to turn away from anything that is preventing us from worshiping and obeying God wholeheartedly.

Ezekiel 18:30-31 *Turn from your sins! Don't let them destroy you! Put all your rebellion behind you, and get for yourselves a new heart and a new spirit.*
Repentance is our only hope of having new life from God.

Matthew 3:2 *Turn from your sins and turn to God, because the Kingdom of Heaven is near.*

Luke 24:47 *There is forgiveness of sins for all who turn to me.*

Acts 2:37-38 *Peter's words convicted them deeply, and they said to him and to the other apostles, "Brothers, what should we do?" Peter replied, "Each of you must turn from your sins and turn to God, and be baptized in the name of Jesus Christ for the forgiveness of your sins. Then you will receive the gift of the Holy Spirit."*
Repentance is our only hope for forgiveness of sin.

Why is repentance necessary?

Ezekiel 33:12 *The good works of righteous people will not save them if they turn to sin, nor will the sins of evil people destroy them if they repent and turn from their sins.*
Repentance leads to forgiveness of sin.

Jeremiah 5:3 *They are determined, with faces set like stone; they have refused to repent.*
The unrepentant heart rejects God and remains in sin's grasp.

Luke 13:3 *And you will also perish unless you turn from your evil ways and turn to God.*
Jesus taught that without repentance we face judgment.

Luke 15:10 *There is joy in the presence of God's angels when even one sinner repents.*
All heaven rejoices when one sinner repents.

Is repentance a one-time event, or do I need to repent each time I sin?

Psalm 51:17 *The sacrifice you want is a broken spirit. A broken and repentant heart, O God, you will not despise.*

Though salvation is a one-time event, God is pleased by broken and contrite hearts that are willing to continually confess and repent of sin.

1 John 1:8-9 *If we say we have no sin, we are . . . refusing to accept the truth. But if we confess our sins to him . . .*

Confession and repentance of sin is a constant mark of the person walking in the light of fellowship with God.

PROMISE FROM GOD: Jeremiah 3:22 *Come back to me, and I will heal your wayward hearts.*

Resentment

(*see also* BITTERNESS)

What causes feelings of resentment?

2 Samuel 6:16 *But as the Ark of the Lord entered the City of David, Michal, the daughter of Saul, looked down from her window. When she saw King David leaping and dancing before the Lord, she was filled with contempt for him.*

Disagreement over conduct can cause resentment.

Genesis 27:36 *Esau said bitterly, "No wonder his name is Jacob, for he has deceived me twice, first taking my birthright and now stealing my blessing. Oh, haven't you saved even one blessing for me?"* Being deceived can cause resentment.

Genesis 4:3-5, 8 *At harvesttime Cain brought to the Lord a gift of his farm produce, while Abel brought several choice lambs from the best of his flock. The Lord accepted Abel and his offering, but he did not accept Cain and his offering. This made Cain very angry and dejected. . . . Later Cain suggested to his brother, Abel, "Let's go out into the fields." And while they were there, Cain attacked and killed his brother.* Jealousy can cause resentment.

Luke 15:27-30 *"Your brother is back," he was told, "and your father has killed the calf we were fattening and has prepared a great feast. We are celebrating because of his safe return." The older brother was angry and wouldn't go in. His father came out and begged him, but he replied, "All these years I've worked hard for you and never once refused to do a single thing you told me to. And in all that time you never gave me even one young goat for a feast with my friends. Yet when this son of yours comes back after squandering your money on prostitutes, you celebrate by killing the finest calf we have."* Feeling left out can cause resentment.

Genesis 37:2-4 *When Joseph was seventeen years old, he often tended his father's flocks with his half brothers, the sons of his father's wives Bilhah and Zilpah. But Joseph reported to his father some of the bad things his brothers were doing. Now Jacob loved Joseph more than any of his other children because Joseph had been born to him in his old age. So one day he gave Joseph a special gift—a beautiful robe. But his brothers hated Joseph because of their father's partiality. They couldn't say a kind word to him.* Favoritism can cause resentment.

What is the danger of resentment?

Job 5:2 *Surely resentment destroys the fool, and jealousy kills the simple.*

Proverbs 27:3 *A stone is heavy and sand is weighty, but the resentment caused by a fool is heavier than both.*

Resentment is both self-destructive and destructive for those we resent. Resentment destroys relationships.

How do I handle my feelings of resentment?

James 5:9 *Don't grumble about each other, my brothers and sisters, or God will judge you.*

1 Thessalonians 5:15 *See that no one pays back evil for evil, but always try to do good to each other and to everyone else.*

Mark 11:25 *But when you are praying, first forgive anyone you are holding a grudge against, so that your Father in heaven will forgive your sins, too.*

Proverbs 10:12 *Hatred stirs up quarrels, but love covers all offenses.*

If resentment has built up, you must pray for God's strength to love and forgive until it forces the resentment from your heart. This is an area where believers can demonstrate to the world that God's power can make a difference.

How can I hope to avoid feelings of resentment in the future?

Leviticus 19:17-18 *Do not nurse hatred in your heart. . . . Never seek revenge or bear a grudge against anyone, but love your neighbor as yourself.*

Matthew 5:43-47 *You have heard that the law of Moses says, "Love your neighbor" and hate your enemy. But I say, love your enemies! Pray for those who persecute you!*

Your heart and mind must be transformed by the love of almighty God.

PROMISE FROM GOD: Mark 11:25 *But when you are praying, first forgive anyone you are holding a grudge against, so that your Father in heaven will forgive your sins, too.*

Safety

(*see also* PROTECTION)

Does God protect those who love him from physical harm?

Daniel 6:22 *My God sent his angel to shut the lions' mouths so that they would not hurt me.*

Psalm 91:11 *For he orders his angels to protect you wherever you go.*
Sometimes God protects and delivers in miraculous ways in order to preserve us so we can continue to serve him.

2 Corinthians 12:7 *I was given a thorn in my flesh, a messenger from Satan to torment me and keep me from getting proud.*
At other times even God's chosen servants experience devastating physical hardship and suffering. These are the times when our faith is put to the test and we must not lose our eternal perspective.

Romans 5:3 *We can rejoice, too, when we run into problems and trials.*
When God does not prevent suffering, he promises strength to endure through the Holy Spirit. Enduring suffering may bring us closer to God than being spared from suffering.

If an accident, tragedy, or illness occurs, does it mean God is punishing me for something?

John 9:3 *"It was not because of his sins or his parents' sins," Jesus answered. "He was born blind so the power of God could be seen in him."*

God is better understood not as the cause of your suffering but as the redeemer of your suffering. Suffering can take you toward God or away from God. If suffering takes you toward God, it is redemptive.

If God doesn't guarantee physical safety, what's the point of faith?

2 Timothy 1:12 *For I know the one in whom I trust, and I am sure that he is able to guard what I have entrusted to him until the day of his return.*

Faith is trusting God to guard and keep that which is eternal—our souls.

1 Peter 3:18 *He died for sinners that he might bring us safely home to God.*

Faith in Christ gives us safe passage to our eternal home.

Is it wrong to pray for safety for myself and my loved ones?

Acts 12:5 *But while Peter was in prison, the church prayed very earnestly for him.*

God always welcomes the confession of your desires when offered in submission to his will.

Romans 1:10 *One of the things I always pray for is the opportunity, God willing, to come at last to see you.* Paul's desire for safety in travel was rooted in his desire to minister to others.

PROMISE FROM GOD: Psalm 34:7 *For the angel of the Lord guards all who fear him, and he rescues them.*

Salvation

What does it mean to be saved?

Romans 4:8 *What joy for those whose sin is no longer counted against them by the Lord.*

Romans 3:24 *Yet now God in his gracious kindness declares us not guilty.*
Being saved means no longer having our sins count against us but rather being forgiven by the grace of God. Being saved does not spare us from earthly troubles, but it does spare us from eternal judgment.

Psalm 103:12 *He has removed our rebellious acts as far away from us as the east is from the west.*
Being saved means our sins have been completely removed.

Psalm 51:9-10 *Remove the stain of my guilt. Create in me a clean heart, O God.*
Being saved means the stain of guilt has been

268

washed away. Guilt not only appears to be gone, it is gone!

Romans 3:24 He has done this through Christ, who has freed us by taking away our sins.
Being saved means we are forgiven in Christ and are assured of eternal life in heaven. What greater hope could we have?

Is salvation available to anyone? How can I be saved?

Romans 10:13 Anyone who calls on the name of the Lord will be saved.
God's Word promises salvation to anyone who calls on Jesus' name.

John 3:16 For God so loved the world that he gave his only Son, so that everyone who believes in him will not perish but have eternal life.
Jesus himself promised that those who believe in him will be saved.

How can I be sure of my salvation?

1 Peter 1:5 And God, in his mighty power, will protect you until you receive this salvation.
You can be sure of your salvation because God has promised that you are saved.

Romans 8:14 For all who are led by the Spirit of God are children of God.
The Holy Spirit takes up residence in your heart and assures you that you are God's child.

Why is salvation necessary?

Genesis 6:11, 13 *Now the earth had become corrupt in God's sight. . . . So God said to Noah, "I have decided to destroy all living creatures."*

Romans 6:23 *For the wages of sin is death.*
Salvation is necessary because sin against a holy God separates us from him, bringing judgment and spiritual death.

Acts 4:12 *There is salvation in no one else! There is no other name in all of heaven for people to call on to save them.*
Although it may sound exclusive, the Bible's claim of "one way" to salvation is actually an expression of the grace and kindness of God.

What is the connection between salvation and hope?

John 3:6 *Humans can reproduce only human life, but the Holy Spirit gives new life from heaven.*
Salvation brings the hope of real and lasting change in our lives.

Romans 5:1 *Since we have been made right in God's sight by faith, we have peace with God.*
Salvation brings the hope of a daily relationship with God. Salvation is not merely a future rescue from sin but a present relationship with God.

Ephesians 2:10 *He has created us anew in Christ Jesus, so that we can do the good things he planned for us long ago.*

Salvation brings the hope of a meaningful life filled with virtue and service. Salvation changes today's footsteps and tomorrow's destiny.

1 Thessalonians 5:10 *He died for us so that we can live with him forever, whether we are dead or alive at the time of his return.*
For those who are saved, even death holds the promise of hope. Although death is considered our worst enemy, it is death that helps us graduate into our eternal reward.

PROMISE FROM GOD: Isaiah 1:18 *No matter how deep the stain of your sins, I can remove it. I can make you as clean as freshly fallen snow.*

Satisfaction

(*see also* CONTENTMENT)

Does God promise to satisfy all my needs?
Proverbs 30:8 *Give me just enough to satisfy my needs.*
God's first work is often to temper and redefine your needs. There is a vast difference between your needs and wants. Don't confuse the two.

Psalm 17:15 *When I awake, I will be fully satisfied, for I will see you face to face.*
Spiritual maturity finds satisfaction in intimacy with God.

Matthew 5:3 *God blesses those who realize their need for him, for the Kingdom of Heaven is given to them.*
Jesus promised that the heart hungry for righteousness will be satisfied. Be sure to keep up your spiritual appetite.

PROMISE FROM GOD: Psalm 107:9 *For he satisfies the thirsty and fills the hungry with good things.*

Security

(*see also* PROTECTION or SALVATION or SAFETY)

With so much change and instability in the world, how does my faith bring security?

Psalm 125:1 *Those who trust in the Lord are as secure as Mount Zion; they will not be defeated but will endure forever.*

Proverbs 1:33 *But all who listen to me will live in peace and safety, unafraid of harm.*

Matthew 7:24 *Anyone who listens to my teaching and obeys me is wise, like a person who builds a house on solid rock.*

Psalm 40:2 *He set my feet on solid ground and steadied me as I walked along.*

When you build your life on God's truth, you have a solid foundation that will not crack under the world's pressure. The Christian's safety and security is rooted deeply in the Lord's presence. With him you can face life with great courage. Without him you stand alone.

How does God provide security?

Psalm 63:8 *I follow close behind you; your strong right hand holds me securely.*

Proverbs 18:10 *The name of the Lord is a strong fortress; the godly run to him and are safe.*

Psalm 46:1-3 *God is our refuge and strength, always ready to help in times of trouble. So we will not fear, even if earthquakes come and the mountains crumble into the sea. Let the oceans roar and foam. Let the mountains tremble as the waters surge!*

Psalm 57:1 *Have mercy on me, O God, have mercy! I look to you for protection. I will hide beneath the shadow of your wings until this violent storm is past.*

Psalm 3:3 *But you, O Lord, are a shield around me, my glory, and the one who lifts my head high.* No matter how much the storms of life batter us, we are eternally secure with God. Nothing can ever separate us from his eternal presence.

How can I feel secure about the future?

Philippians 4:6-7 *Don't worry about anything;*

instead, pray about everything. . . . If you do this, you will experience God's peace, which is far more wonderful than the human mind can understand.

Your greatest security comes from knowing the peace of God through prayer.

Romans 8:39 *Nothing in all creation will ever be able to separate us from the love of God.*

The most powerful security in the world is knowing that nothing can separate you from the love of God.

Revelation 3:5 *All who are victorious will be clothed in white. I will never erase their names from the Book of Life, but I will announce before my Father and his angels that they are mine.*

God has promised to save us when we accept his Son, Jesus Christ, as our Savior. God always keeps his promises. When Jesus holds us securely, Satan cannot get his hands on us.

PROMISES FROM GOD: Romans 8:39 *Whether we are high above the sky or in the deepest ocean, nothing in all creation will ever be able to separate us from the love of God.*

Titus 3:7 *He declared us not guilty because of his great kindness. And now we know that we will inherit eternal life.*

Sickness

(*see also* HEALING)

Does God care when I am sick?

Psalm 41:3 *The Lord nurses them when they are sick and eases their pain and discomfort.*

Philippians 2:27 *And he surely was ill; in fact, he almost died. But God had mercy on him—and also on me, so that I would not have such unbearable sorrow.*

Matthew 4:23 *Jesus traveled throughout Galilee teaching in the synagogues, preaching everywhere the Good News about the Kingdom. And he healed people who had every kind of sickness and disease.*

Revelation 21:4 *He will remove all of their sorrows, and there will be no more death or sorrow or crying or pain. For the old world and its evils are gone forever.*

Our compassionate, merciful God has full authority over all sickness. He can heal whomever he chooses. He can grant his authority to heal to whomever he chooses. Eventually, he will remove all sickness and suffering from all of his children for eternity. Sometimes he chooses not to heal a person, even a devout Christian. We do not understand why, but someday we will understand.

What is a positive way I can respond in times of personal sickness?

Psalm 103:2-3 *Praise the Lord, I tell myself, and never forget the good things he does for me. He forgives all my sins and heals all my diseases.* Praise the Lord for his ability to forgive your sins and heal your diseases—even if he chooses not to heal you. Praise the Lord when he uses your infirmities to move you closer to him.

James 5:14 *Are any among you sick? They should call for the elders of the church and have them pray over them, anointing them with oil in the name of the Lord.*

Proverbs 17:22 *A cheerful heart is good medicine, but a broken spirit saps a person's strength.* Ask the Lord for healing and be content with his decision. The Lord may choose not to heal you so he can use you more effectively.

Psalm 73:26 *My health may fail, and my spirit may grow weak, but God remains the strength of my heart; he is mine forever.*

1 Corinthians 15:43 *Our bodies now disappoint us, but when they are raised, they will be full of glory. They are weak now, but when they are raised, they will be full of power.* Regardless of the condition of your health, whether you are well or sick, you can rejoice that God faithfully remains your strength. Your frail

276

earthly body will one day be gloriously transformed for eternity.

How can I minister to the sick?

James 5:14-15 *Are any among you sick? They should call for the elders of the church and have them pray over them, anointing them with oil in the name of the Lord. And their prayer offered in faith will heal the sick, and the Lord will make them well. And anyone who has committed sins will be forgiven.*
You can pray for those who are sick. Some will be healed and some will be strengthened spiritually when they are not healed.

John 5:7 *"I can't, sir," the sick man said, "for I have no one to help me into the pool when the water is stirred up. While I am trying to get there, someone else always gets in ahead of me."*

Mark 2:3-5 *Four men arrived carrying a paralyzed man on a mat. They couldn't get to Jesus through the crowd, so they dug through the clay roof above his head. Then they lowered the sick man on his mat, right down in front of Jesus. Seeing their faith, Jesus said to the paralyzed man, "My son, your sins are forgiven."*
You can help the sick receive healing.

Luke 10:33-34 *Then a despised Samaritan came along, and when he saw the man, he felt deep pity. Kneeling beside him, the Samaritan soothed his wounds with medicine and bandaged them. Then he put the man on his own donkey and took him to an inn, where he took care of him.*

Matthew 25:36 *I was naked, and you gave me clothing. I was sick, and you cared for me. I was in prison, and you visited me.*
You can meet the physical, emotional, social, and spiritual needs of the sick.

Why does God heal some and not others?

John 9:3, 7 *"It was not because of his sins or his parents' sins," Jesus answered. "He was born blind so the power of God could be seen in him.". . . He told him, "Go and wash in the pool of Siloam" (Siloam means Sent). So the man went and washed, and came back seeing!*

John 11:4-6 *But when Jesus heard about it he said, "Lazarus's sickness will not end in death. No, it is for the glory of God. I, the Son of God, will receive glory from this." Although Jesus loved Martha, Mary, and Lazarus, he stayed where he was for the next two days and did not go to them.*

Psalm 119:71 *The suffering you sent was good for me, for it taught me to pay attention to your principles.*

Romans 5:3 *We can rejoice, too, when we run into problems and trials, for we know that they are good for us—they help us learn to endure.*
God possesses the ability to heal all diseases. He heals, or does not heal, for reasons we cannot

always comprehend right now. But we do know that God's love for us is greater than the greatest love any human being has had for another. And it is because of this great love for us that he is preparing a place in heaven where sickness will be gone forever.

PROMISE FROM GOD: Isaiah 58:11 *The Lord will guide you continually, watering your life when you are dry and keeping you healthy, too. You will be like a well-watered garden, like an ever-flowing spring.*

Sin

(*see also* FORGIVENESS or REPENTANCE)

What is sin?

Romans 3:23 *All have sinned; all fall short of God's glorious ideal.*
Sin is falling short of the standards of a holy God.

Romans 2:15 *They demonstrate that God's law is written within them, for their own consciences either accuse them or tell them they are doing what is right.*
Sin is violating God's moral law.

Ephesians 2:2 *You used to live just like the rest of the world, full of sin, obeying Satan.*
Sin, in its most basic element, is obedience to Satan.

Is everyone sinful?

Psalm 14:3 *All have turned away from God; all have become corrupt. No one does good, not even one!*

Ecclesiastes 7:20 *There is not a single person in all the earth who is always good and never sins.*

Isaiah 53:6 *All of us have strayed away like sheep. We have left God's paths to follow our own.*

Psalm 51:5 *I was born a sinner—yes, from the moment my mother conceived me.*

We are all born sinful. It is a condition at birth, not a practice we cultivate.

Jeremiah 17:9 *The human heart is most deceitful and desperately wicked. Who really knows how bad it is?*

The human heart is far more sinful than we want to believe.

How can I be free from sin's guilt and power?

Psalm 51:2-3 *Wash me clean from my guilt. Purify me from my sin. For I recognize my shameful deeds—they haunt me day and night.*

Psalm 139:23-24 *Search me, O God, and know my heart; test me and know my thoughts. Point out anything in me that offends you, and lead me along the path of everlasting life.*

Ask God to cleanse your heart from sin.

Isaiah 1:18 *"Come now, let us argue this out," says the Lord. "No matter how deep the stain of your sins, I can remove it. I can make you as clean as freshly fallen snow. Even if you are stained as red as crimson, I can make you as white as wool."*

M a t t h e w   2 6 : 2 8 *For this is my blood, which seals the covenant between God and his people. It is poured out to forgive the sins of many.*

2   C o r i n t h i a n s   5 : 2 1 *For God made Christ, who never sinned, to be the offering for our sin, so that we could be made right with God through Christ.*

H e b r e w s   9 : 1 4 *Just think how much more the blood of Christ will purify our hearts from deeds that lead to death so that we can worship the living God.* God has made it possible for the stain of your sin to be removed through the death and resurrection of the Lord Jesus Christ.

E z r a   1 0 : 1 1 *Confess your sin to the Lord, the God of your ancestors, and do what he demands.*

1   J o h n   1 : 9 *But if we confess our sins to him, he is faithful and just to forgive us and to cleanse us from every wrong.*
Confessing your sins to God and turning away from them to obey God is the way to a right relationship with him. When you confess your sins to God and turn away from them, he forgets them and forgives you.

G a l a t i a n s   5 : 2 4 *Those who belong to Christ Jesus have nailed the passions and desires of their sinful nature to his cross and crucified them there.*

Because of what Christ has done, those who have faith in God are free from the power of sin. This doesn't mean you will no longer sin, but that sin's power over you has been defeated.

Am I really a Christian if I still sin?

Romans 7:20 *But if I am doing what I don't want to do, I am not really the one doing it; the sin within me is doing it.*
You will always struggle with sin, but in Christ you are guaranteed the victory.

1 John 3:9 *Those who have been born into God's family do not sin. . . . They can't keep on sinning.*
Although believers will still sin, by God's grace you do not have to be dominated by the practice of sin. True believers in Christ no longer cling tenaciously to sin.

Romans 8:5 *But those who are controlled by the Holy Spirit think about things that please the Spirit.*
Sin loses its influence over you as you increasingly yield your life to the control of the Holy Spirit. The Spirit of God living in you reduces your appetite for sin and increases your hunger for God.

What can I do when I become aware of sin in my life?

2 Corinthians 7:9 *Now I am glad I sent it, not because it hurt you, but because the pain caused you to . . . change your ways.*

James 4:9 *Let there be tears for the wrong things you have done.*

1 John 1:9 *But if we confess our sins to him, he is faithful and just to forgive us.*
Confession of sin brings the cleansing of forgiveness.

PROMISES FROM GOD: Proverbs 28:13 *People who cover over their sins will not prosper. But if they confess and forsake them, they will receive mercy.*

Isaiah 1:18 *No matter how deep the stain of your sins, I can remove it.*

Sorrow

(*see also* ENCOURAGEMENT)

I have trouble reconciling the sorrow and grief of life with the love of God. Is God concerned about my pain?
Isaiah 53:3 *He was despised and rejected—a man of sorrows.*
Through the pain and sorrow of Christ's experiences on earth, God has experienced the depths of human grief.

John 11:35-36 *Then Jesus wept. The people who were standing nearby said, "See how much he loved him."*

The tears of Jesus demonstrate that great grief comes from great love.

Luke 19:41 *But as they came closer to Jerusalem and Jesus saw the city ahead, he began to cry.*
Jesus grieves when those he loves do not respond to his offer of salvation.

1 Peter 5:7 *Give all your worries and cares to God, for he cares about what happens to you.*
God cares not only about your eternal future, but also about your present troubles.

How can I find hope in my times of sorrow?

Psalm 30:5 *Weeping may go on all night, but joy comes with the morning.*

John 16:20 *You will grieve, but your grief will suddenly turn to wonderful joy when you see me again.*

Revelation 21:4 *He will remove all of their sorrows, and there will be no more death or sorrow or crying or pain.*
God promises to relieve your weeping and replace it with his joy.

2 Corinthians 1:4 *He comforts us in all our troubles so that we can comfort others.*
Those who have received the comfort of Christ in the midst of grief become a comforting presence to others.

PROMISE FROM GOD: Revelation
2 1 : 4 *He will remove all of their sorrows, and there
will be no more death or sorrow or crying or pain. For
the old world and its evils are gone forever.*

Spiritual Disciplines

(*see also* PRAYER)

Are the spiritual disciplines really important?

Mark 1:35 *The next morning Jesus awoke long
before daybreak and went out alone into the wilderness to pray.*

Luke 5:16 *But Jesus often withdrew to the wilderness for prayer.*

Matthew 4:2 *For forty days and forty nights he
ate nothing and became very hungry.*
The spiritual disciplines were central to Jesus'
earthly life. If the Son of God needed them, so
do we.

What are some benefits of meditating on Scripture?

Psalm 19:8 *The commandments of the Lord are
right, bringing joy to the heart. The commands of the
Lord are clear, giving insight into life.*
Knowing and reflecting on God's Word will

increase our joy and our understanding of the perplexities of life, for God counsels us through his Word.

Psalm 119:105 *Your word is a lamp for my feet and a light for my path.*
The Bible gives us the resources to make wise decisions, for in it is God's wisdom itself.

What is the purpose of fasting?

Acts 13:2-3 *One day as these men were worshiping the Lord and fasting, the Holy Spirit said, "Dedicate Barnabas and Saul for the special work I have for them." So after more fasting and prayer, the men laid their hands on them and sent them on their way.*
Fasting signifies that God is our top priority and hunger for God is more important to us than hunger for food. Thus fasting is often coupled with prayer and seeking God's guidance.

Joel 2:12 *That is why the Lord says, "Turn to me now, while there is time! Give me your hearts. Come with fasting, weeping, and mourning."*
Fasting is associated with humbling ourselves in God's presence.

What is the purpose of prayer?

2 Chronicles 7:14 *Then if my people who are called by my name will humble themselves and pray and seek my face and turn from their wicked ways,*

I will hear from heaven.
Prayer is an act of humble worship in which we
seek God with all our hearts.

1 John 1:9 *But if we confess our sins to him,*
he is faithful and just to forgive us and to cleanse
us from every wrong.
Prayer involves confession of sin.

Psalm 9:1-2 *I will thank you, Lord, with all*
my heart. . . . I will sing praises to your name,
O Most High.
Through prayer we praise our mighty God.

What is the purpose of solitude?

1 Kings 19:8-9 *So he got up and ate and drank,*
and the food gave him enough strength to travel forty
days and forty nights to Mount Sinai, the mountain
of God. There he came to a cave, where he spent the
night. But the Lord said to him, "What are you doing
here, Elijah?"
In solitude, we abandon the distractions of life
and things we have come to depend on that
deceive us into believing we can make it on our
own. When we stand alone, face-to-face with
God, we realize how much we need him and
depend on him.

Can spiritual disciplines be misused?

Matthew 6:7 *When you pray, don't babble on*
and on as people of other religions do. They think

their prayers are answered only by repeating their words again and again.

We misuse the spiritual disciplines if we think we can use them to get leverage with God or to force God to bless us.

Matthew 6:16 *And when you fast, don't make it obvious, as the hypocrites do, who try to look pale and disheveled so people will admire them for their fasting. I assure you, that is the only reward they will get.*

We misuse the spiritual disciplines if we do them only to seek praise for our spirituality.

Isaiah 58:3 *"We have fasted before you!" they say. "Why aren't you impressed? We have done much penance, and you don't even notice it!" "I will tell you why! It's because you are living for yourselves even while you are fasting. You keep right on oppressing your workers."*

We misuse the spiritual disciplines when we act as if they are an end in themselves rather than a means to godly living.

PROMISE FROM GOD: Jeremiah 29:13 *If you look for me in earnest, you will find me when you seek me.*

Strength

What is the evidence of God's strength?

Psalm 65:6 *You formed the mountains by your power and armed yourself with mighty strength.*

Romans 1:20 *From the time the world was created, people have seen the earth and sky and all that God made. They can clearly see his . . . eternal power.*
God's mighty power is evident in creation.

Psalm 66:5-7 *Come and see what our God has done, what awesome miracles he does for his people!*
God's people recognize his powerful works. Every sunrise and sunset speaks of his majesty. Every snowflake reveals his creativity. Every fruit and berry is a symbol of his provision.

Acts 9:21 *All who heard him were amazed. "Isn't this the same man who persecuted Jesus' followers?"*
A life transformed by the gospel of Christ is evidence of God's power.

How can I experience the strength of God in my life?

Ephesians 1:19 *I pray that you will begin to understand the incredible greatness of his power for us who believe him.*
The power of the Resurrection is experienced by all who trust Christ for salvation. The power

of the Resurrection is the mighty power of God over death itself.

How can I become stronger in my faith?

Judges 6:27 *So Gideon . . . did as the Lord had commanded.*
You grow in faith when you obey God's call.

Joshua 3:8 *When you reach the banks of the Jordan River, take a few steps into the river and stop.*
When you step out in faith, you begin to experience God's power. Faith is not stagnant but active.

1 Thessalonians 3:2 *We sent him to strengthen you, to encourage you in your faith.*
You grow stronger through the mutual encouragement and accountability of other believers.

Jude 20 *Continue to build your lives on the foundation of your holy faith. And continue to pray as you are directed by the Holy Spirit.*
The Holy Spirit strengthens your faith through prayer.

PROMISES FROM GOD: Nehemiah 8:10 *The joy of the Lord is your strength!*

Isaiah 40:29, 31 *He gives power to those who are tired and worn out; he offers strength to the weak. . . . Those who wait on the Lord will find new strength.*

Stress

(*see also* ADVERSITY or PRESSURE)

How can I deal with stress?

Psalm 55:22 *Give your burdens to the Lord, and he will take care of you. He will not permit the godly to slip and fall.*

Psalm 62:2 *He alone is my rock and my salvation, my fortress where I will never be shaken.*

Matthew 11:28 *Come to me, all of you who are weary and carry heavy burdens, and I will give you rest.*
Recognize that God brings true peace of heart and mind. The first step in dealing with stress is to bring your burdens to the Lord.

Psalm 86:7 *I will call to you whenever trouble strikes, and you will answer me.*
Be persistent in prayer.

2 Corinthians 4:9 *We are hunted down, but God never abandons us. We get knocked down, but we get up again and keep going.*
Be aware that problems and pressures are inevitable. But even in the midst of them, God is invincible.

Mark 6:31 *Then Jesus said, "Let's get away from the crowds for a while and rest." There were so many people coming and going that Jesus and his apostles didn't even have time to eat.*

Make time to slow down and take a break from pressure-packed situations.

Galatians 6:9 *Don't get tired of doing what is good. Don't get discouraged and give up, for we will reap a harvest of blessing at the appropriate time.* Deal with stress. Don't let stress defeat you. When you are tired of doing good, it may be because you are just too tired.

Our true character is exposed when we are under stress. How do I respond to stress so that something good can come from it?

James 1:2-4 *Dear brothers and sisters, whenever trouble comes your way, let it be an opportunity for joy. For when your faith is tested, your endurance has a chance to grow. So let it grow, for when your endurance is fully developed, you will be strong in character and ready for anything.* Character is built from the positive building blocks of life. But it is also built from conquering the stresses and problems of life. What you do with stress not only reveals your character but also helps develop your character.

PROMISE FROM GOD: John 16:33 *I have told you all this so that you may have peace in me. Here on earth you will have many trials and sorrows. But take heart, because I have overcome the world.*

Suffering

Why do I experience suffering?

Genesis 37:28 *So when the traders came by, his brothers pulled Joseph out of the pit and sold him for twenty pieces of silver.*

Joshua 7:1 *A man named Achan had stolen some of these things, so the Lord was very angry with the Israelites.*

2 Samuel 15:13-14 *A messenger soon arrived in Jerusalem to tell King David, "All Israel has joined Absalom in a conspiracy against you!" "Then we must flee at once, or it will be too late!" David urged his men.*

Sometimes you suffer because of the sins of others, not your own sins.

Job 1:19 *The house collapsed, and all your children are dead.*

John 9:2-3 *"Teacher," his disciples asked him, "why was this man born blind? Was it a result of his own sins or those of his parents?" "It was not because of his sins or his parents' sins," Jesus answered.*

Sometimes the suffering that comes to you is not your fault. It just happens. In this case, how you react to the suffering is the key.

Proverbs 3:11-12 *My child, don't ignore it when the Lord disciplines you. . . . For the Lord*

corrects those he loves, just as a father corrects a
child in whom he delights.
Sometimes God sends suffering as punishment
for your sins. He disciplines you because he
loves you and wants to correct you and restore
you to him.

Deuteronomy 8:2 *Remember how the Lord*
your God led you through the wilderness for forty
years, humbling you and testing you . . . to find out
whether or not you would really obey his commands.
Sometimes God tests you with suffering to
encourage you to obey him.

James 1:3 *For when your faith is tested, your*
endurance has a chance to grow.
Sometimes you suffer because it will help you
grow and mature.

2 Timothy 3:12 *Yes, and everyone who wants to*
live a godly life in Christ Jesus will suffer persecution.
The world hates Christ; so when you identify
with him, you can expect the world that inflicted
suffering on him to also inflict suffering on you.

Does God care when I am suffering?

Psalm 23:4 *Even when I walk through the dark*
valley of death, I will not be afraid, for you are close
beside me. Your rod and your staff protect and
comfort me.
God sticks with you even in your most intense
suffering.

Psalm 56:8 *You keep track of all my sorrows. You have collected all my tears in your bottle. You have recorded each one in your book.*
Your suffering matters to God because *you* matter to God.

Can any good come from my suffering?

Job 5:17-18 *But consider the joy of those corrected by God! Do not despise the chastening of the Almighty when you sin. For though he wounds, he also bandages. He strikes, but his hands also heal.*
Suffering can bring great renewal and healing if it drives you to God.

Romans 5:3-4 *We can rejoice, too, when we run into problems and trials, for we know that they are good for us—they help us learn to endure. And endurance develops strength of character.*

Hebrews 12:11 *No discipline is enjoyable while it is happening—it is painful! But afterward there will be a quiet harvest of right living for those who are trained in this way.*

James 1:3-4 *For when your faith is tested, your endurance has a chance to grow. . . . When your endurance is fully developed, you will be strong in character and ready for anything.*

2 Corinthians 1:5 *You can be sure that the more we suffer for Christ, the more God will shower us with his comfort through Christ.*

2 Corinthians 12:10 *Since I know it is all for Christ's good, I am quite content with my weaknesses and with insults, hardships, persecutions, and calamities. For when I am weak, then I am strong.*
When suffering is for your good, Christ's glory, and the building of his church, you should be happy to accept it.

2 Corinthians 1:3-4 *All praise to the God and Father of our Lord Jesus Christ. He is the source of every mercy and the God who comforts us. He comforts us . . . so that we can comfort others.*
Suffering enables you to give comfort to others.

How do I stay close to God in times of suffering?

Psalm 22:24 *For he has not ignored the suffering of the needy. He has not turned and walked away. He has listened to their cries for help.*
Recognize that God has not abandoned you in times of suffering.

Psalm 126:5-6 *Those who plant in tears will harvest with shouts of joy. They weep as they go to plant their seed, but they sing as they return with the harvest.*
Recognize that suffering is not forever. In the dark hours of the night of suffering it is hard to think of a morning of joy and gladness. But the tears of suffering are like seeds of joy.

Matthew 17:12 *And soon the Son of Man will also suffer at their hands.*

Hebrews 2:18 *Since he himself has gone through suffering and temptation, he is able to help us when we are being tempted.*
Recognize that Jesus himself suffered for you. Christ suffered the agonies of the cross, which not only embraced incredible physical suffering but also the unthinkable suffering of bearing the sins of the world.

Romans 8:17-18 *And since we are his children, we will share his treasures—for everything God gives to his Son, Christ, is ours too. But if we are to share his glory, we must also share his suffering. Yet what we suffer now is nothing compared to the glory he will give us later.*
Recognize that all suffering will end forever when those who believe in Jesus are welcomed into heaven.

How can I respond to the suffering of others?

1 Corinthians 12:26 *If one part suffers, all parts suffer with it, and if one part is honored, all the parts are glad.*
When one Christian suffers, it should hurt us all, for we are all members of Christ's body— unified. If one part of our body hurts, it sets up sympathetic pain throughout our entire body. So it should be in the body of Christ. If you know someone who is hurting, suffer along with that person.

Romans 12:15 *When others are happy, be happy with them. If they are sad, share their sorrow.* Suffering people need empathy, not advice.

PROMISES FROM GOD: Psalm 147:3 *He heals the brokenhearted, binding up their wounds.*

Zechariah 9:12 *Come back to the place of safety, . . . for there is yet hope! I promise this very day that I will repay you two mercies for each of your woes!*

Sympathy

Does the Lord really sympathize with me in my time of need?

Psalm 103:13-14 *The Lord is like a father to his children, tender and compassionate to those who fear him. For he understands how weak we are; he knows we are only dust.*
There is no trouble that comes to you without the watchful eye of your heavenly Father seeing it and sympathizing with you. To know that he knows is the beginning of healing.

Matthew 9:36 *He felt great pity for the crowds that came, because their problems were so great and they didn't know where to go for help. They were like sheep without a shepherd.*

Luke 7:13 *When the Lord saw her, his heart overflowed with compassion. "Don't cry!" he said.*

Hebrews 4:15 *This High Priest of ours understands our weaknesses, for he faced all of the same temptations we do, yet he did not sin.*
The story of Jesus is a story of tender compassion toward those in need. There is no temptation, hurt, or pain that comes into your life without touching the sympathetic heart of Jesus. Jesus knows and cares.

How can I show sympathy to others?
Luke 10:36-37 *"Now which of these three would you say was a neighbor to the man who was attacked by bandits?" Jesus asked. The man replied, "The one who showed him mercy." Then Jesus said, "Yes, now go and do the same."*
By helping the person in need.

2 Corinthians 1:4 *When others are troubled, we will be able to give them the same comfort God has given us.*
By sharing words of encouragement.

PROMISE FROM GOD: 1 Peter 3:8 *Finally, all of you should be of one mind, full of sympathy toward each other, loving one another with tender hearts and humble minds.*

Temptation

(*see also* TESTING)

Is being tempted to sin the same as sinning?

Hebrews 4:15 *[Jesus] faced all of the same temptations we do, yet he did not sin.*
Jesus was often tempted, yet he never gave in to the temptations. Therefore, since Jesus was sinless, being tempted is not the same as sinning. We don't have to feel guilty about the temptations we wrestle with. Rather, we can devote ourselves to resisting them.

How can I avoid falling into temptation?

Genesis 39:12 *He ran from the house.*
If possible, remove yourself from the tempting situation.

Proverbs 1:10 *If sinners entice you, turn your back on them!*
Sometimes your greatest tempters are those you think are your friends. If you know you are liable to give in to the pressure of certain people, it is best to avoid their company.

Daniel 1:8 *But Daniel made up his mind not to defile himself by eating the food.*
A solid commitment made before temptation strikes is the best preventive to sin.

Ecclesiastes 4:12 *A person standing alone can be attacked and defeated, but two can stand back-to-back and conquer. Three are even better, for a triple-braided cord is not easily broken.*
Enlisting a Christian friend as an accountability partner will give you far more spiritual strength than you have on your own.

Genesis 3:6 *The fruit looked so fresh and delicious. . . . So she ate some.*

1 Kings 11:1, 3 *Solomon loved many foreign women. . . . And sure enough, they led his heart away from the Lord.*
Recognize Satan's strategy of making sin look attractive and beneficial. Let your actions be governed not by your feelings but by the Word of God.

Does temptation ever come from God?

James 1:13 *God is never tempted to do wrong, and he never tempts anyone else either.*

Mark 7:15 *You are defiled by what you say and do!*
Temptation originates not in the mind of God but within our own hearts. But victory over temptation originates not in our hearts but in the mind of God.

PROMISES FROM GOD: Psalm 1:1
Oh, the joys of those who do not follow the advice of the wicked.

1 Corinthians 10:13 *But remember that the temptations that come into your life are no different from what others experience. And God is faithful. He will keep the temptation from becoming so strong that you can't stand up against it. When you are tempted, he will show you a way out so that you will not give in to it.*

Terrorism

(*see also* FEAR)

How can I avoid living in constant fear?

Psalm 27:1 *The Lord is my light and my salvation—so why should I be afraid? The Lord protects me from danger—so why should I tremble?*
Trusting that God is in control of the world, that he is all-powerful, and that he will one day judge all people and punish the wicked can free you from crippling fear.

Matthew 10:28 *Don't be afraid of those who want to kill you. They can only kill your body; they cannot touch your soul.*
Remembering that your eternity is secure in Christ and untouchable by terrorists can build your confidence.

Does living by faith mean I should not take precautions?

Acts 9:29-30 *He debated with some Greek-speaking Jews, but they plotted to murder him. When the believers heard about it, however, they took him to Caesarea and sent him on to his hometown of Tarsus.*

Faith is different from foolhardiness. God often gives us the wisdom to take precautions. Take such actions not because you are overcome by terror but because you are acting wisely.

How should I pray in this time of terrorism?

Psalm 7:6 *Arise, O Lord, in anger! Stand up against the fury of my enemies! Wake up, my God, and bring justice!*

It is appropriate to be outraged by acts of terrorism and to pray that God will protect you and bring terrorists to justice.

Matthew 5:43-44 *You have heard that the law of Moses says, "Love your neighbor" and hate your enemy. But I say, love your enemies! Pray for those who persecute you.*

You can pray that terrorists will find God's love and that their lives will be transformed. This is complementary, not contradictory, to the prayer that God will judge terrorists.

Matthew 6:10 *May your Kingdom come soon. May your will be done here on earth, just as it is in heaven.*

It is important to pray not just against terrorism,

but for God's purposes, and to look forward to the fulfillment of God's kingdom at the return of Jesus.

PROMISE FROM GOD: Isaiah 41:10 *Don't be afraid, for I am with you. Do not be dismayed, for I am your God. I will strengthen you. I will help you. I will uphold you with my victorious right hand.*

Testing

(*see also* TEMPTATION)

What good comes out of being tested?

Jeremiah 6:27 *Jeremiah, I have made you a tester of metals, that you may determine the quality of my people.*
Spiritual testing reveals the impurities and sins of our hearts. Once we recognize our shortcomings, we can let God forgive and remove them.

Deuteronomy 13:3 *The Lord your God is testing you to see if you love him with all your heart and soul.*
God's testing results in a deepening of our obedience and love.

Luke 8:13 *The rocky soil represents those who hear the message with joy. But like young plants in such soil, their roots don't go very deep. They believe* for a while, but they wilt when the hot winds of testing blow.

Testing reveals the strength of our commitment.

How is a test different from a temptation?

1 Peter 1:7 *These trials are only to test your faith, to show that it is strong and pure.*

Whereas Satan tempts to destroy our faith, God tests to strengthen and purify.

James 1:3 *For when your faith is tested, your endurance has a chance to grow.*

Temptations, when resisted with God's help, become tests that purify our character.

PROMISE FROM GOD: James 1:12 *God blesses the people who patiently endure testing. Afterward they will receive the crown of life that God has promised to those who love him.*

Thankfulness

What can I be thankful for?

Mark 6:41 *Jesus took the five loaves and two fish, looked up toward heaven, and asked God's blessing on the food.*

You can thank God for his provision of life's basic needs, such as food, clothing, shelter, oxygen, and life itself.

Psalm 13:5-6 *But I trust in your unfailing love. I will rejoice because you have rescued me. I will sing to the Lord because he has been so good to me.*
You can thank God for helping you through your troubles.

James 1:17 *Whatever is good and perfect comes to us from God above, who created all heaven's lights. Unlike them, he never changes or casts shifting shadows.*
You can thank God for everything good in your world and in your life.

Are there things I can be thankful for even when circumstances are not going well?

1 Chronicles 16:34 *Give thanks to the Lord, for he is good! His faithful love endures forever.*

Psalm 7:17 *I will thank the Lord because he is just; I will sing praise to the name of the Lord Most High.*

Psalm 138:2 *I bow before your holy Temple as I worship. I will give thanks to your name for your unfailing love and faithfulness, because your promises are backed by all the honor of your name.*
You can thank the Lord for being good and just. You can thank him for his unchanging, perfect character. You can thank him also for his love for you, his faithfulness, for sending his Son, Jesus, for his mercy. You can thank him for victory over death and for keeping his promises.

How can I develop an attitude of thanksgiving?

Psalm 136:24-26 *He saved us from our enemies. His faithful love endures forever. He gives food to every living thing. His faithful love endures forever. Give thanks to the God of heaven. His faithful love endures forever.*

Discipline yourself to make some time every day for thanksgiving. Make a mental list of God's blessings in your life—especially the most recent ones—and thank him for them. Don't wait to feel thankful before giving thanks. Giving thanks will lead you to feel thankful.

What are some good ways to express my thankfulness?

Psalm 147:7 *Sing out your thanks to the Lord; sing praises to our God, accompanied by harps.*

Colossians 3:16 *Sing psalms and hymns and spiritual songs to God with thankful hearts.*

With music and singing.

Psalm 100:4 *Enter his gates with thanksgiving; go into his courts with praise. Give thanks to him and bless his name.*

By praising and honoring the Lord.

Psalm 116:17 *I will offer you a sacrifice of thanksgiving.*

Through worship and giving.

Colossians 4:2 *Devote yourselves to prayer with an alert mind and a thankful heart.*

Psalm 111:1-2 *Praise the Lord! I will thank the Lord with all my heart as I meet with his godly people. How amazing are the deeds of the Lord! All who delight in him should ponder them.*

PROMISE FROM GOD: Psalm 147:1 *Praise the Lord! How good it is to sing praises to our God! How delightful and how right.*

Timing of God

How was Jesus' life an example of God's perfect timing?

Galatians 4:4 *But when the right time came, God sent his Son, born of a woman, subject to the law.*

John 7:30 *Then the leaders tried to arrest him; but no one laid a hand on him, because his time had not yet come.*

Romans 5:6 *When we were utterly helpless, Christ came at just the right time and died for us sinners.*

The Hebrew people had been longing for the Messiah for centuries, yet God sent Jesus to earth at just the right time. We won't fully understand why this was perfect timing until we get to heaven and see God's complete plan. But we can be assured that God sent Jesus at the time when the most people would be reached with the Good News of salvation, both present and future.

Ephesians 1:10 *And this is his plan: At the right time he will bring everything together under the authority of Christ—everything in heaven and on earth.*

If Jesus' first coming was timed exactly right, we can be confident that Jesus' second coming will be right on schedule.

What are other examples of God's perfect timing?

Exodus 6:1 *"Now you will see what I will do to Pharaoh," the Lord told Moses. "When he feels my powerful hand upon him, he will let the people go. In fact, he will be so anxious to get rid of them that he will force them to leave his land!"*

Exodus 9:16 *But I have let you live for this reason—that you might see my power and that my fame might spread throughout the earth.*

Exodus 12:36 *The Lord caused the Egyptians to look favorably on the Israelites, and they gave the Israelites whatever they asked for. So, like a victorious army, they plundered the Egyptians!*

John 11:14-15, 21, 32, 43-45 *Then he told them plainly, "Lazarus is dead. And for your sake, I am glad I wasn't there, because this will give you another opportunity to believe in me. Come, let's* go see him.". . . *Martha said to Jesus, "Lord, if you had been here, my brother would not have died.". . . When Mary arrived and saw Jesus, she fell down at his feet and said, "Lord, if you had been here, my brother would not have died.". . . Then Jesus shouted, "Lazarus, come out!" And Lazarus came out, bound in graveclothes, his face wrapped in a headcloth. Jesus told them, "Unwrap him and let him go!" Many of the people who were with Mary believed in Jesus when they saw this happen.*

The Lord's rescue of Israel from Egypt and Jesus' raising of Lazarus show how God's timing, while sometimes confusing at first, always works out for the best. The same will be true in your life.

How can I be patient as I wait for God's timing?

Psalm 31:5 *I entrust my spirit into your hand. Rescue me, Lord, for you are a faithful God.*

Psalm 59:9 *You are my strength; I wait for you to rescue me, for you, O God, are my place of safety.* Remind yourself continually of God's faithfulness. He is actively working in your life to help you become all he made you to be.

Psalm 69:13 *But I keep right on praying to you, Lord, hoping this is the time you will show me favor. In your unfailing love, O God, answer my prayer with your sure salvation.*

Be steadfast in prayer.

PROMISE FROM GOD: Habakkuk
2:3 *But these things I plan won't happen right
away. Slowly, steadily, surely, the time approaches
when the vision will be fulfilled. If it seems slow, wait
patiently, for it will surely take place. It will not be
delayed.*

Tired

Why am I so tired?

Job 7:3 *I, too, have been assigned months of
futility, long and weary nights of misery.*
You may be tired because you have a long
sickness and are growing weary of it.

2 Corinthians 11:27 *I have lived with weariness and pain and sleepless nights. Often I have been
hungry and thirsty and have gone without food. Often
I have shivered with cold, without enough clothing
to keep me warm.*
You may be tired because you are constantly
lacking necessary resources.

Proverbs 23:4-5 *Don't weary yourself
trying to get rich. Why waste your time? For riches
can disappear as though they had the wings of
a bird!*
You may be tired because you are striving too
hard for something that isn't worth it.

2 Corinthians 5:2 *We grow weary in our present bodies, and we long for the day when we will put on our heavenly bodies.*
You may be tired because your body is aging and slowing down. As we grow older or face sickness or infirmity, we grow weary of our failing bodies and long for the new bodies we shall receive in heaven.

1 Samuel 14:24 *Now the men of Israel were worn out that day, because Saul had made them take an oath, saying, "Let a curse fall on anyone who eats before evening—before I have full revenge on my enemies." So no one ate a thing all day.*
You may be tired because you are not eating well.

Ecclesiastes 12:12 *But, my child, be warned: There is no end of opinions ready to be expressed. Studying them can go on forever and become very exhausting!*
You may be tired because you are not seeing the end of a project, a desire, or an answer to prayer.

Psalm 40:2 *He lifted me out of the pit of despair, out of the mud and the mire.*
You may be tired because you are depressed or discouraged.

Psalm 31:10 *I am dying from grief; my years are shortened by sadness. Misery has drained my strength; I am wasting away from within.*
You may be tired because grief has drained your strength.

Who can help me when I grow tired and weary?

Isaiah 40:29-31 *He gives power to those who are tired and worn out; he offers strength to the weak. Even youths will become exhausted, and young men will give up. But those who wait on the Lord will find new strength. They will fly high on wings like eagles. They will run and not grow weary. They will walk and not faint.*

2 Corinthians 12:9 *Each time he said, "My gracious favor is all you need. My power works best in your weakness." So now I am glad to boast about my weaknesses, so that the power of Christ may work through me.*

Matthew 11:28 *Then Jesus said, "Come to me, all of you who are weary and carry heavy burdens, and I will give you rest."*
The Lord who gives you strength will also renew your strength.

What do I have to watch out for when I'm tired?

Galatians 6:9 *So don't get tired of doing what is good. Don't get discouraged and give up, for we will reap a harvest of blessing at the appropriate time.*
Being tired makes you more susceptible to discouragement, temptation, and sin and causes you to lose hope that things will ever change.

Proverbs 30:1-2 *I am weary, O God; I am weary and worn out, O God. I am too ignorant to be human, and I lack common sense.*
Being tired causes you to lose your perspective.

Job 10:1 *I am disgusted with my life. Let me complain freely.*
Being tired can cause you to say things you may later regret.

Ecclesiastes 1:8 *Everything is so weary and tiresome! No matter how much we see, we are never satisfied.*
Being tired can cause you to lose your vision and purpose.

Nehemiah 4:10 *Then the people of Judah began to complain that the workers were becoming tired.*

2 Samuel 17:1-2 *Now Ahithophel urged Absalom, "Let me choose twelve thousand men to start out after David tonight. I will catch up to him while he is weary and discouraged. He and his troops will panic, and everyone will run away. Then I will kill only the king."*
Weariness makes you vulnerable to temptations and enemies. It causes you to lose your confidence and trust in God.

PROMISE FROM GOD: Psalm 145:14 *The Lord helps the fallen and lifts up those bent beneath their loads.*

Trust

(*see also* ASSURANCE and FAITH)

What makes God trustworthy?

T i t u s 1 : 2 *This truth gives them the confidence of eternal life, which God promised before the world began—and he cannot lie.*
We can trust God because he always tells the truth.

L a m e n t a t i o n s 3 : 2 2 *The unfailing love of the Lord never ends!*

R o m a n s 5 : 8 *But God showed his great love for us by sending Christ to die for us while we were still sinners.*
We can trust God because God loves us and therefore always has our best interests at heart. The supreme guarantee of God's love is the sacrifice of his Son for us so that we might live forever with him in heaven.

M a l a c h i 3 : 6 *I am the Lord, and I do not change.*
We can trust God because he is eternally unchanging. We never have to worry whether his character or attitude toward us will be different tomorrow.

What does it mean to trust God?

P s a l m 3 3 : 2 1 *In him our hearts rejoice, for we are trusting in his holy name.*

Trusting God means recognizing that God is trustworthy and then trusting him above all else.

Genesis 6:14, 17, 22 *"Make a boat. . . . I am about to cover the earth with a flood.". . . Noah did everything exactly as God had commanded him.*
Trusting God means obeying his commands even when we don't fully understand.

Galatians 2:16 *For no one will ever be saved by obeying the law.*
Trusting Christ for salvation means ceasing to trust in our own efforts to be righteous.

1 Peter 1:8 *Though you do not see him, you trust him.*
Trusting God means being confident in him even though we can't see him.

PROMISES FROM GOD: Isaiah 26:3 *You will keep in perfect peace all who trust in you, whose thoughts are fixed on you!*

Matthew 25:29 *To those who use well what they are given, even more will be given.*

1 Corinthians 1:9 *God will surely do this for you, for he always does just what he says.*

Hebrews 10:23 *God can be trusted to keep his promise.*

Victory

What does it mean to live a "victorious Christian life"?

1 J o h n 5 : 4 *For every child of God defeats this evil world by trusting Christ to give the victory.*
If we are willing, God will help us defeat sin in our lives.

1 C o r i n t h i a n s 9 : 2 6 *So I run straight to the goal with purpose in every step.*
To experience victory in the Christian life we must be willing to commit ourselves to vigorous spiritual training and preparation.

P s a l m 9 8 : 2 *The Lord has announced his victory and has revealed his righteousness to every nation!*

R o m a n s 8 : 3 7 *Overwhelming victory is ours through Christ, who loved us.*

1 C o r i n t h i a n s 1 5 : 5 7 *How we thank God, who gives us victory over sin and death through Jesus Christ our Lord!*
Our greatest victory is receiving God's gift of salvation, which has been won by Christ.

Does faith promise that we will all be winners?

1 C o r i n t h i a n s 1 : 2 7 *And he chose those who are powerless to shame those who are powerful.*
As believers we may not be "winners" by the

world's standards, but we have been chosen for glory by God.

PROMISE FROM GOD: John 16:33
Take heart, because I have overcome the world.

War

(*see also* PEACE)

What does God think of war?

Psalm 116:15 *The Lord's loved ones are precious to him; it grieves him when they die.*

God created every person and God loves every person. Therefore anything that takes human life grieves God. So, even if we conclude there are times when war is permissible or necessary, remember that war should always be our last resort. And it is wise to be careful about glorifying war and reveling in death—even the death of our enemies.

Will God ever do anything about war?

Micah 4:3 *The Lord will settle international disputes. All the nations will beat their swords into plowshares and their spears into pruning hooks. All wars will stop, and military training will come to an end.*

Psalm 46:8-9 *Come, see the glorious works of the Lord: See how he brings destruction upon the world and causes wars to cease throughout the earth. He breaks the bow and snaps the spear in two; he burns the shields with fire.*

When Jesus returns, war will be abolished forever. This is a cause for comfort and joy.

PROMISE FROM GOD: Matthew 5:9 *God blesses those who work for peace, for they will be called the children of God.*

Wisdom

How will having wisdom help me?

Ecclesiastes 10:10 *Since a dull ax requires great strength, sharpen the blade. That's the value of wisdom; it helps you succeed.*

Wisdom will help you to succeed in what you do. So if you want to fail, reject God's wisdom.

Ephesians 5:15 *Be careful how you live, not as fools but as those who are wise.*

Wisdom helps you know how to live.

1 Kings 3:9 *Give me an understanding mind so that I can govern your people well and know the difference between right and wrong.*

The more responsibility you have, the more

of God's wisdom you need in order to do what is right.

Proverbs 3:21-26 My child, don't lose sight of good planning and insight. Hang on to them, for they fill you with life and bring you honor and respect. They keep you safe on your way and keep your feet from stumbling. You can lie down without fear and enjoy pleasant dreams. You need not be afraid of disaster or the destruction that comes upon the wicked, for the Lord is your security. He will keep your foot from being caught in a trap.
Wisdom will help preserve you from trouble and disaster.

1 Corinthians 1:19 I will destroy human wisdom and discard their most brilliant ideas.
Spiritual wisdom allows you to know the difference between what the Bible says is wise and what the world claims to be wise.

Is wisdom something I can learn or acquire—or do I have to be born with it?

Proverbs 4:5 Learn to be wise, and develop good judgment.
You learn wisdom; it is not inborn.

1 Kings 3:9 Give me an understanding mind so that I can . . . know the difference between right and wrong.
Solomon prayed for wisdom and God gave it to him.

Does old age produce wisdom?

Job 32:7-9 *I thought, "Those who are older should speak, for wisdom comes with age." Surely it is God's Spirit within people, the breath of the Almighty within them, that makes them intelligent. But sometimes the elders are not wise. Sometimes the aged do not understand justice.*

We do well to remember that life experience does not automatically produce wisdom. It is life experience, filtered through a teachable spirit, prayerfully linked to the truths of Scripture, that gives one the full spiritual benefit of old age.

How do I obtain wisdom?

James 1:5 *If you need wisdom . . . ask him, and he will gladly tell you. He will not resent your asking.* God promises to give wisdom to anyone who asks.

Job 28:28 *The fear of the Lord is true wisdom; to forsake evil is real understanding.*

Giving God first place in your life is a prerequisite for God's guidance. Asking God for wisdom is a hollow request if you are not willing to let God rule in your heart. Wisdom comes from having a relationship with God.

1 John 2:27 *But you have received the Holy Spirit, and he lives within you, so you don't need anyone to teach you what is true. For the Spirit teaches you all things, and what he teaches is true—*

it is not a lie. So continue in what he has taught you, and continue to live in Christ.

You find wisdom in the context of a relationship with God. When you are willing to be the learner, the Holy Spirit is willing to be your Teacher.

Proverbs 8:12, 17 *I, Wisdom, live together with good judgment. I know where to discover knowledge and discernment. . . . I love all who love me. Those who search for me will surely find me.*

You find wisdom when you seek it single-mindedly and wholeheartedly. Like many of the best things in life, to find wisdom you must pursue it.

Proverbs 20:18 *Plans succeed through good counsel; don't go to war without the advice of others.*

Wisdom often comes to you through the counsel of thoughtful, godly people.

Psalm 119:98 *Your commands make me wiser than my enemies, for your commands are my constant guide.*

God's Word is an unending source of wisdom for those who apply themselves to study it.

PROMISE FROM GOD: Proverbs 1:23 *Come here and listen to me! I'll pour out the spirit of wisdom upon you and make you wise.*

Index

If you enjoyed *TouchPoints of Hope*, you will love the *TouchPoint Bible*.

The *TouchPoint Bible* is the most helpful Bible available for finding just the right Bible verses to meet an immediate need in your life or in the life of someone you are trying to help. With the exclusive HelpFinder Index, you have instant access to hundreds of key topics and thousands of Bible verses. The *TouchPoint Bible* also includes book introductions and Bible promises as well as hundreds of in-text application notes to help you apply God's truth to everyday life. Make the *TouchPoint Bible* your favorite Bible for church, devotional reading, or study.